W4

99

99

When just 18, Danni Murray had to decide between going to law school and entering the working world. She chose the latter and moved from her hometown on the Gold Coast to Sydney. She was soon signed with Vivien's Models and eventually Ford Model Agency in New York, embarking on a career as a professional high-fashion model.

The next exciting step was being signed to BMG Arista as a vocal recording artist. Danni worked with an Australian producer for two years and appeared as co-host at the Arias, with Bon Jovi, in 1992. Danni is listed as one of the original "pop divas" of Australia. She later worked with producers in the UK as a solo artist and travelled extensively.

Danni was flying back from Australia to the USA when she started talking to an established Manhattan interior designer. Seeing her excitement, the designer offered her an intern position.

The next three years were spent working under the watchful eye of her mentor, whilst studying at NYU. This enabled Danni to learn the principles of a successful design business, along with the opportunity to develop her own unique sense of style.

Meeting an Englishman while in New York, who would later become her husband, another continent beckoned. After settling in Chelsea, London, Danni embedded herself in the UK with the launch of a new business – Star PR. With revenues of over one million pounds sterling in the first year, the agency became one of the London's largest event management and PR staffing companies at the time.

Married, with one son, Danni soon became pregnant for the second time and made the decision to move the family back home to Sydney. Star PR was sold to a competitor.

During this pregnancy, Danni graduated with honours from the International School of Colour and Design and won a recognition award for one of her designs. A third boy in the family was born the next year. A series of house moves with her growing family brought renovation and client design projects aplenty in Sydney.

Purchasing a magnificent farmhouse in Berry, NSW, allowed her to turn creative theory into practice in her very own property. The finished property was published in several magazines and later sold.

Soon after, Danni decided to take her knowledge and start up on her own. She launched The Clifton Club, specialising in luxury accommodation letting, event management and interior design. With nearly 50 homes on the books nationwide, she assisted with interior styling and solely-managed events for high-profile individuals. Building a cutting-edge reputation, more high-end interior/event-based work naturally evolved outside of the Clifton Club.

Tending to her fourth child and requiring a more homebased set-up, Danni consolidated her work as a successful freelance interior/events decorator and launched her own interior design business in 2011, ELK&MAPLE. Her style is upmarket "homely", with a passion for colonial, folk and country American architecture.

Her design business gained momentum and in 2014, Danni introduced her own homewares collection, called SYRUP. A gap in the market presented itself while she was trying to source fitting products to include in her interior design projects.

After a two-year development process, the wares were launched at a trade fair in Sydney and later featured both online and in her pop-up store "Teepee. The Store", on the Upper North Shore, which traded for one year. The design business Danni manages under the banner of Teepee Creative is celebrating nineteen years in business this year.

She resides on a semi-rural property on the Northern Beaches with her husband, four boys, chickens, horses and a dog named Daisy May.

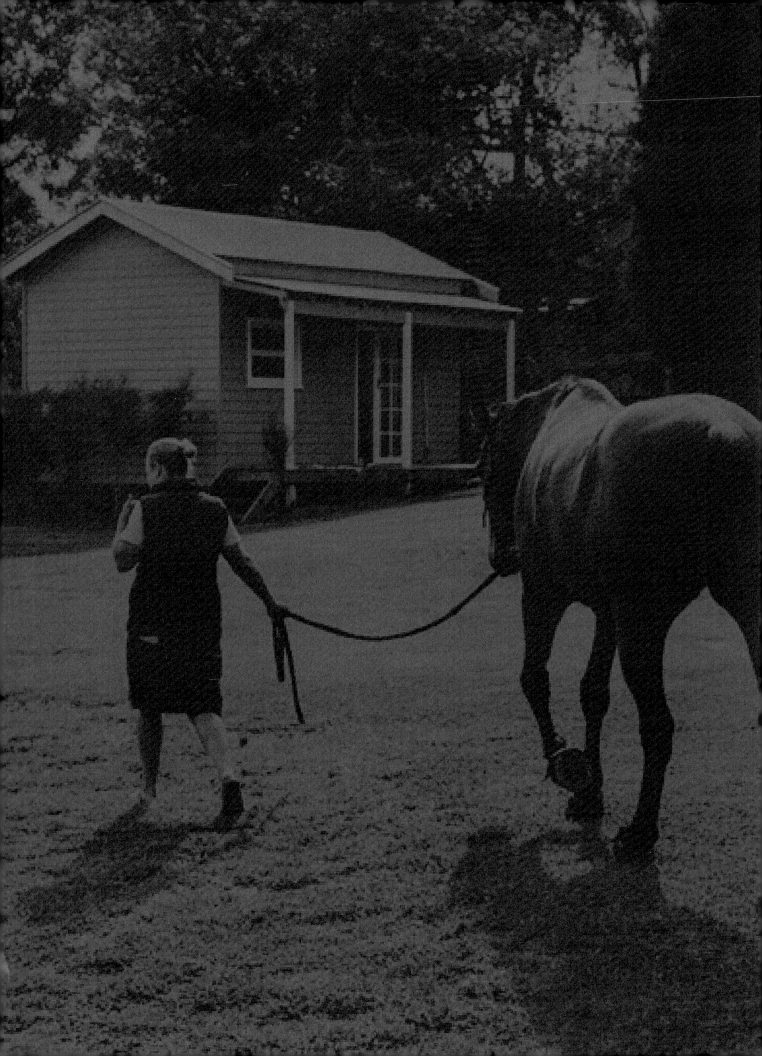

A FARMHOUSE AND A FAMOUS KANGAROO

WITH PHOTOGRAPHY - TOBI MURRAY & FELIX FOREST

DANNI MURRAY

AUSTIN MACAULEY PUBLISHERS™
LONDON • CAMBRIDGE • NEW YORK • SHARJAH

A CIP catalogue record for this title is available from the British Library.

ISBN 9781398433427 (Hardback)
ISBN 9781398433434 (ePub e-book)

www.austinmacauley.com

First Published 2022
Austin Macauley Publishers Ltd®
1 Canada Square
Canary Wharf
London
E14 5AA

To Australians, past, present and future, whether Aboriginal, European, Antipodean, Asian, or of other origins.

In unity, let our appreciation of what we have reflect equality, sustainability and the utmost respect for each other.

To my boys – I hope the roundtable research at dinner time remains strong in your memory and that you value this resource as a legacy to pass down to many more generations to come.

And to my husband, this lifestyle you have provided us is appreciated more than you will ever know. We are lucky to have you.

I love you all so much.

So much appreciation for Jennifer Lancaster, who has patiently helped me through the phases of first-time editing. You were a fabulous teacher. I would like to sincerely acknowledge the neighbourhood in which I am fortunate enough to reside in, and the community members who embraced me during writing this book. Special thanks to the Terrey Hills Library for the wonderful original articles and photographs. Absolute treasure. Much of the content included in the book feels like I was simply a communicative vessel for the stories that needed to be left as legacies. I feel enormously privileged to have a greater understanding of the area I live in, and amazing people who choose to call the area home.

Table of Contents

Tribute to Nancy Hill Wood

April 26 1941 – August 5 2016

A child of the Stolen Generation, an ambassador to Indigenous People, a proud member of the Bundjalung Tribe and a much-loved local.

In 1967, Nancy and her husband, Tony, settled on the Northern Beaches of New South Wales. Nancy, born in Kyogle Northern New South Wales in 1941, lost her Mother soon after she was born. Motherless, Nancy was taken away from her Father at six months of age, and placed into a children's home in Bomaderry, Nowra. This home was run by Christian Missionaries. It was the first home established by Christian Missionaries, and is now a heritage site. It is also known as the birthplace of the children from the Stolen Generation. Nancy lived there until she was twelve and then moved to Cootamundra Girls' Training Home to learn how to be a domestic worker. At eighteen, with a very limited education but well trained in domesticity, Nancy was put out to work as a domestic servant. She arrived to embark on her placement in Sydney by train.

Whilst working as a domestic servant in Sydney, Nancy met Tony Wood, and they were married in 1967.

Nancy and Tony later adopted and raised five aboriginal children in Terrey Hills, named John, Raelene, Suzie, Rodney and Sasha. She lived on the Northern Beaches for over 50 years. Nancy studied at Sydney's Tranby National Indigenous Adult College. In 1999, Nancy launched her first book of poetry titled, "Nobody's Child."In 2005 Nancy chaired the NSW Sorry Day Committee.

Nancy became a strong voice for her community regularly speaking at various forums about her extraordinary life in the past as a child of the Stolen Generation.

Nobody's Child

A shadow within a little girl
A nothing, a misery.
Within me to stay

Not knowing the feeling that's in my heart.
Her soul is sad at she knows no love.
No care, no cuddles.
No comforting word.
Surrounded around me
My brothers and Sisters
And yet I can't see

A smile on their faces.
No joy in their voices
Nor sound of their laughter
They look on our faces

So sad and forlorn.
The stolen generation.
Kidnapped from happiness

A Mum and Dad we never knew
Still lingers in my heart.
The place where we were born
One day we will return.

It may be sad and sorrow
When we hear the real truth
Of what had really happened

(NOBODY'S CHILD a poem by NANCY HILL WOOD)

SYDNEY, NSW - MAY 26: Sixty-five-year-old, Nancy Hill Wood, one of the "Stolen Generation", attends an event to mark Sorry Day May 26, 2006 in Sydney, Australia. The first National Sorry Day was held on 26 May 1998 - one year after the tabling of the report "Bringing them Home" which was the result of an inquiry into the forced removal of Aboriginal and Torres Strait Islander children - the "Stolen Generation" – from their parents, families, communities and culture.

Preface

When I first started out in the interior design industry, I would often be fixated on a certain concept, colour scheme or vibe I'd created for a client. But as I grew into my own interior design skin, I reminded myself to let a project "evolve." I've learned to start with a good foundation and direction, but be led by the path of the unknown, allowing creativity to shine at its best.

It's 2021; one of our country's worst years in terms of natural disasters. From drought, to raging bushfires, to flooding, to then the worldwide phenomenon of coronavirus, we find ourselves having to adjust to suit current environments. There's never been more focus on the importance of our home, friends and family. Highlighted is our need for mutual support, a safe haven of home and a realisation of the strong need for sustainable living.

This book is here to remind us all to trust in our ancestors' past and learn from their fundamental understanding of what a good life entails.

Benefiting from their life skills and experiences, our elders' wisdom should be incorporated into our modern everyday living as a platform for a more sustainable, healthier and happier life in the future. Integrating the knowledge of those who have walked these trails before us, whether that be an indigenous tribe, an Australian living through wartimes or an Italian migrant farmer, is a crucial step in completing our own full-circle personal evolution.

To evolve…it's been a message sent to us loud and clear for a number of years now…it's time to reconnect with Mother Nature and invest in our children's futures. It's time to rebuild a strong sense of community.

If anything, I intended this book as a gift to my boys, with a summary of your family life as kids, and to be used as a reference when, at some point, you just might need to be reminded of your roots.

What an absolute privilege to have collaborated on this with you, Tobi. You have created the most beautiful pictorial curation of our family life here in Duffys Forest and I will always treasure this time spent with you.

Bio: Tobi Murray

Tobias Murray is an undergraduate student at UNSW Art and Design (formerly COFA), majoring in photography. Tobias' portfolio has been built over his university career featuring a diverse range of images inspired by travel, street scenes and studio practice. Tobias has already gained an impressive interest in his skills, with work including press photography for a SONY signed musician, an album cover for a local band along with a featured piece in Australian photography magazine Bendt Magazine.

His latest commission sees Tobias' photography displayed throughout A Farmhouse and a Famous Kangaroo. He aims to continue his existing work, hoping to collaborate alongside editorial creatives with established fashion designers and brands. Tobias has shown his body of works in group showcases and is looking to release his own publication – featuring his latest personal projects – in the near future.

STOP THE AIRFIELD

DO YOU WANT A NORTH SHORE BANKSTOWN?

DO YOU REALISE:—

1. DUFFYS FOREST WILL BECOME AN INDUSTRIAL AREA.

2. .FLIGHT PATHS COULD BE OVER YOUR HOME.

3. LIGHT AIRCRAFT WILL BE NOISY AND LOW.

4. YOUR PEACE WILL BE DESTROYED.

ACT NOW!

1. WRITE TO YOUR LOCAL MEMBER OF PARLIAMENT, C/o. PARLIAMENT HOUSE SYDNEY & CANBERRA. AND TO COUNCILLORS AT SHIRE HALLS.

2. ATTEND THE PUBLIC MEETING AT MONA VALE COMMUNITY HALL ON THURSDAY, 17th JUNE AT 7.30 p.m.

THE NORTH SHORE AERO CLUB WILL STACK THIS MEETING

COME AND "UNSTACK" IT!

F. J. WILLIAMS, PRINTER, TERREY HILLS

Do you believe you will be unaffected by the airfield? If so refer to the map.

F. J. WILLIAMS, PRINTER, TERREY HILLS

DUFFY'S FOREST AIRPORT

Foreword

By Hayley Baillie

I met my dear friend Danni through our combined philanthropic work with the Australian Red Cross. When I found out that Danni lived in Duffys Forest with her four boys, I was excited to share stories of my own childhood growing up down the road.

I moved to Terrey Hills in 1980 when I was eight years old. Dad had found a property of a few acres, bordering Ku-ring-gai National Park, big enough for him to keep his helicopter at home.

My first memories of our block of land in Booligal Road was that we were really going to be living in the bush. We had a horse farrier as our neighbour and a gun club down the road that would keep you on your toes on Wednesday and Saturday afternoons with the sound of gunfire.

When our house was being built in 1979, we were threatened by a bushfire that destroyed our neighbours' home. The bush seemed to regenerate before our eyes, all while my sister Jenny and I went off every day to Terrey Hills Public School.

Being an active schoolgirl and a school captain, one of my favourite things to do each year was to visit the Japanese School's open day, where I loved tasting all the "exotic food." I also fondly remember doing jazz ballet in the school hall.

Those were very different times. There was a nudist colony down the road (next to where the Northern Beaches Christian School is now situated!) and the prestigious Terrey Hills Golf Course was then a brick pit where people rode motorbikes on a dirt jump track.

I learnt to drive a car in the quiet backstreets of Duffy's Forest and I loved the blue light disco nights held in the community centre. My sister Jenny was a keen horse rider and she kept her horse in the stables on our neighbour's property.

Mum and Dad (Dick Smith and Phillipa McManarney) built the Australian Geographic Centre on Mona Vale Road and had a wildlife conservation program as part of the compound. I worked in the subscription department during my school holidays. This building is now home to my favourite Indian restaurant, Urban Tadka.

Hayley and Jenny and a special Joey

A wildlife park in Duffys Forest, where the TV show Skippy was filmed, was a great place to take our overseas friends to visit. In the natural surrounds, they could pat a kangaroo or cuddle a koala.

Dad had worked on the TV series when he was a two-way radio salesman with Weston Electronics and set up the radio equipment that appeared in the series.

At home we had an interesting collection of pets, including three orphan kangaroos, a sheep, two cats, a dog named Buffy, chooks, ducks and the occasional visiting brown snake.

Forty years later, Dad is still flying his helicopter in and out of home base and walks down to Smith's Creek almost every day to be in the bush and get his exercise. My whole family love to get together at Mum and Dad's home in the bush surrounded by the peace and tranquillity of this beautiful part of Sydney.

The Smith family

Who Is Hayley Baillie?

Hayley Baillie is passionate about travel and adventure. As the daughter of Australia's most recognised adventurer, entrepreneur and philanthropist Dick Smith, you might say it's in the blood.

Hayley was exposed from an early age to Dick's passion for Australia, for preserving its natural heritage and showcasing it to the world…not to mention a curiosity for the wild and beautiful planet around us.

As a young adult, Hayley sought adventure for more than a decade as a naturalist guide on board the world's best expedition ships. From the North to the South Pole and oceans in between, she contributed to guests' nature and adventure experiences as an underwater specialist, scuba instructor and film maker.

In 2003, Hayley created Baillie Lodges with life and business partner James Baillie. Their vision was to develop a premium boutique portfolio of accommodation experiences. Additions include luxury lodges on Lord Howe Island, Kangaroo Island and Longitude 131°, the famed desert "camp" overlooking Uluru.

Hayley and partner commissioned works from the Ernabella Arts Inc organisation, then created a mentorship program to support local artists and one ceramicist. Baillie Lodges has since introduced standout locations of unique natural significance, setting new benchmarks for experiential travel.

Hayley is a strong believer in philanthropy and supports a number of charities and not-for-profit initiatives, including the Australian Red Cross Society of Women Leaders, the Australian Ballet and the Australian Marine Conservation Society.

Introduction

When the bailiffs came knocking one stormy Saturday afternoon, after a Managed Investment Scheme we had invested in had collapsed, it was apparent the only way forward financially was not exactly what we had planned.

After this sour investment, we had no option but to sell our "forever" family home perched on the leafy upper North Shore and re-think our future. This hit my husband and I hard.

We had envisaged a solid family future in this grand historical home with dreams of possible wedding celebrations and oodles of grandchildren visiting. The universe had other plans for us.

After reluctantly selling and in the interim, renting, we were at a loss to find a property that instilled that resounding "this is the one" feeling, so we decided to expand our home-hunting horizons.

Trawling for hours through "refined criteria" searches, an entirely new proposition presented itself to us in a place they call Duffys Forest.

After celebrating our success in securing a home in the area, one which we had already redecorated in our imaginations, we were promptly gazumped. We were once again tasked with finding a place to plant our family's roots.

On an impulse late one afternoon, something prompted me to drive out to Duffys Forest, leaving me only just enough time to get there, take a look and then head straight back to make the afternoon school pick up. That whimsical drive re-routed us right into our destiny.

I seemed to be possessed by a direction unbeknownst to myself. On auto-drive, I was taken straight to a house where the agent was literally banging up the for sale sign. I caught myself, as this was the very same agent with whom we had just lost out on a property.

Sometimes karma can bring reciprocal blessings. We viewed the house the very next day, weeks before the scheduled open homes and pretty much bought it on the spot.

Our new postcode was to become 2084, Duffys Forest. A two-year love affair renovating this house was about to unfold, and as it happened, the creation of a semi-rural lifestyle with the added benefit of a wondrous education of the area's bountiful history.

I hope you enjoy this pictorial account of our semi-rural lifestyle in the city of Sydney, Australia, peppered with a historical account of an area with so much Australian significance but known to most as "Skippy the Bush Kangaroo" territory – that became our world.

Danni Murray

Traditional Owners

First of all, I would like to sincerely acknowledge the traditional and rightful owners of the land on which we live.

The people I pay homage to are reputed to belong to the greater tribes of Guringay/Wanangine, but there is a great deal of uncertainty as to the actual name of the tribes who inhabited Duffys Forest to this very day.

This area, from the Hawkesbury River to the North Shore bushlands of Sydney, has long been known as Ku-ring-gai, but in fact, this term was coined by an early anthropologist to name country with no recorded name, out of convenience.

It will take some time, but a movement from the Aboriginal Land Council is rising to reinstate the integrity of tribes that once called this area home.

I pay my respects to the elders, past, present and emerging in this beautiful area I also now get to call home.

Terrey Hills and Duffys Forest are both situated within the beautiful Ku-ring-gai Chase National Parklands. The land is the second largest National Protected Park in New South Wales, at just over 150km2 in size.

The clan name "Guringay" was taken and misspelled by John Fraser in 1892. This word 'Ku-ring-gai' was then attached to a great parcel of land we know currently as Ku-ring-gai National Park.

This aggregation of multiple clan names into one by Fraser is frowned upon by many successors of aboriginal historians. The Guringay Peoples are known to reside in the Newcastle, Port Stephens and up to the Singleton area.

The historical dwelling of the aboriginal inhabitants in this area dates back some 7,500 years. The local language is said to be that of Gringai (Guringai). Our street name translates to "place of peace" in this tongue.

The ancient stone carvings from the original inhabitants are still apparent on certain trails in the bushland within the Terrey Hills/Duffys Forest regions and more are being discovered to this day: a legacy left to remind us of our rich past.

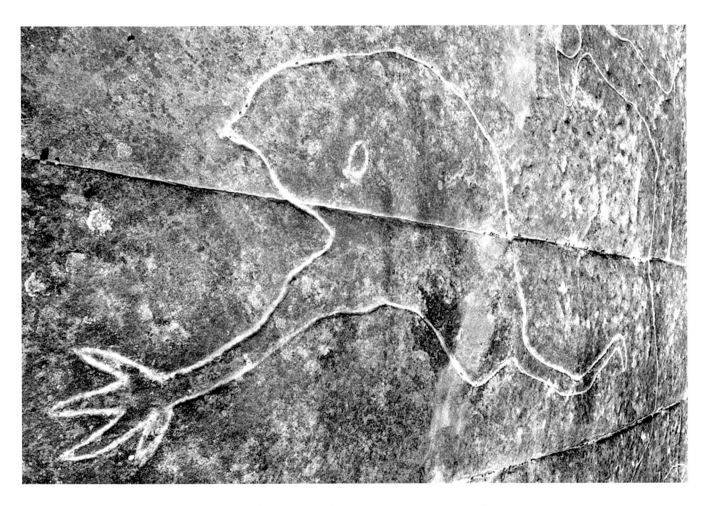

Aboriginal Heritage Council

European Settlement in Guringay

Within three years of arriving in Sydney, Governor Arthur Philip had explored as far as Cowan Creek. Here, he initially had friendly encounters with the Aboriginal people of the area.

As the land became more inhabited by the European settlers, access to the original inhabitants' land and resources diminished. Raging smallpox had an extreme impact on the local Aboriginal population. With widespread illness and deaths – along with land seizure and destruction to make way for the European way of farming – the tribe was forced to leave their home and move further afield.

The area is beautifully wooded, so soon attracted the business of lumber after the European settlers discovered the area's vast opportunity in the logging trade.

You might wonder why a suburban area is known as 'Duffys Forest'. An Irish immigrant, Patrick Duffy, arrived in Sydney in 1822 with his family on board a ship named Eliza (Later, this became the name of one of his daughters). He had served in the "Buffs" (Royal East Kent Regiment – British Army) for around twenty years, got shot in the leg a couple of times, married and had seven children in total.

Then a corporal, he was originally posted to Hobart, taking charge of the convict settlements but was soon instructed to return to Sydney. Duffy spent the next eighteen years raising his family and awaiting instruction from his commanding officers.

After much time had passed and by then suffering rheumatism from the wounds of war, Duffy applied for discharge. In 1830, he appealed for land as a reward for his services.

The land he was awarded was 100 acres, now known as Thornleigh.

In 1857, after a dispute of land ownership with another ex-serviceman, that he won, Duffy cut a road through to Cowan Creek. This lane is now named Duffy Avenue and is the cutting that led him to the area of Duffys Forest.

The Duffy timber business was in full swing and he needed infrastructure to transport his timber out, slowly by horse and carriage on the road or a quicker trip by barge. Thus, Duffys Wharf was built on Cowan Creek and still stands today. Horse-drawn carts were eventually changed to bullocks to cope with heavy loads. The road used for transporting the logs, albeit now modernised, is also still in existence, and connects the rest of Sydney to Duffys Forest.

Duffys Forest was known for lumber, citrus, flowers and its tight-knit community during the late 1800s and early 1900s.

Guringay has been protected as an area of natural beauty from 1894, all because of Frederick Eccleston Du Faur, a Turramurra resident, who campaigned by taking the NSW Governor on a visit to the area. The governor was so impressed that the area was granted an area of natural beauty and protected thereafter.

Little Cottage. behind
Surrey Hills Cement Store
Carnegie Estate Agency.
Surrey Hills

MINISTER FOR LANDS

NEW SOUTH WALES

SYDNEY.

11th March, 1953.

R.W. Askin, Esq., M.L.A.,
Parliament House,
SYDNEY.

Dear Mr. Askin,

I desire to acknowledge
your personal representations on behalf
of the Terrey Hills Progress Association
(Mr. F. Beckman, Hon. Secretary, Myoora
Road, Terrey Hills), requesting further
information in relation to 5 acre blocks.

I shall look into this
matter and let you have advice as soon
as possible.

Yours faithfully,

(F.H. Hawkins)
Minister for Lands.

PARENTS AND CITIZENS' ASSOCIATION

TERREY HILLS

AFFILIATED WITH THE FEDERATION OF PARENTS & CITIZENS' ASSOCIATIONS
OF NEW SOUTH WALES

PRESIDENT:
Mr. R.D. Newland.

HON. SECRETARY:
Mrs. L.M. Rhodes.

Booralie Rd.,
TERREY HILLS.
8th August, '52.

The Secretary,
Terrey Hills Progress Assn.,
TERREY HILLS.

Dear Sir,

In reply to your letter dated 21st. ult. I have to advise
that Mr. J. Thistleton has been authorised to speak on behalf of
this Assn. at your next meeting, with regard to transport.

As you are no doubt aware the 9.15 am. Terrey Hills/Chatswood
bus now takes the children along Myoora Rd., direct to the school,
but our request that the 3.8 pm. Chatswood/Belrose be extended, was
not put into effect.

At our last meeting I was asked to join you in waiting on the
Minister for Transport should you still desire to do so.

It was also resolved, on the motion of Mrs. Curry, to ask
that you apply for Booralie Rd., to be tarred, to enable the bus service
to be extended to the end of the road, in order to give better transport
to the school children living in that area.

Awaiting your reply.

Yours faithfully,

PARENTS & CITIZENS ASSN
TERREY HILLS

G.Rhodes

Hon. Sec.

THE PARLIAMENT OF THE COMMONWEALTH.

56 Lauderdale Avenue,
MANLY. N.S.W.

2nd August, 1950.

Dear Mrs. Simington,

As you will realise, the question of
roads is more a matter for the State Government and the
Council than it is for the Federal Government.

However, I am naturally interested in it,
even if only indirectly and will do anything I can within
my limited powers to help you.

I have sent a copy of your letter to both
Mr. Askin, the State Member and the President of the Warringah
Shire Council.

During the next few days I shall be at Terrey
Hills myself and shall make a personal inspection of the area.

I know the difficulties all road construction
authorities are having with this heavy rain but I agree
with you that this is not the whole story.

With all good wishes and hoping that
something will be done to cure the present conditions,

Yours sincerely,

(W.C. WENTWORTH)

Mrs. H. Simington,
"Ukurrie",
Cooyong Road,
TERREY HILLS. N.S.W.

ADDRESS YOUR REPLIES
TO HONORARY SECRETARY

Parents & Citizens'
Association

THE HOME OF THE WARATAH

Terrey Hills

NEW SOUTH WALES

SYDNEY'S HEALTHIEST & MOST PROGRESSIVE SUBURB, OVERLOOKING
THE SEA AND 700 FEET ABOVE IT. BETWEEN ST. IVES & MONA VALE

Farming

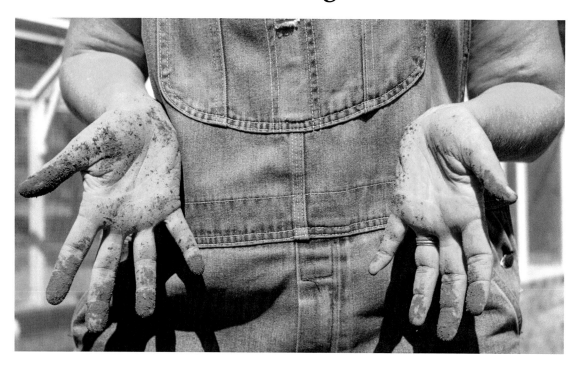

Even though an Italian presence in Sydney's Northern Beaches is recorded well before the 1920s, it wasn't till the 1940s that the major influx of Italians occurred.

The government's migration Populate or Perish scheme attracted Italian migrants to our shores and the Northern Beaches of Sydney became heavily populated with Italian farmers looking for a better life.

The Australian government promised new homes to 20,000 Italians each year, for a five-year period from 1945. Our country required more manpower to help with heavy construction projects (Snowy Mountains Hydro Scheme for example), along with a need to reverse the rapidly declining birth rate due to Australian war casualties.

And reverse it did! The population doubled in one year and we now have at least one million Australians who claim to have some kind of Italian background. During the time of the Italian increase in population, word was sent back home that life in Australia was a good life and the Italian population only continued to increase as a result with families independently moving here.

The very first market gardens managed by Italian immigrants were nestled in Dee Why and Beacon Hill in the 1940s (A descendant of the very first Italian family still resides in Beacon Hill.) The Northern Beaches became popular for market gardens, while areas such as Duffys Forest were soon discovered as perfect areas for farming and crops.

Crops producing tomatoes, beans, strawberries, peas, cabbage, cauliflower, lettuce and potatoes were established, along with flowers and fresh eggs. Fruit and vegetable shops run by these families were a natural progression.

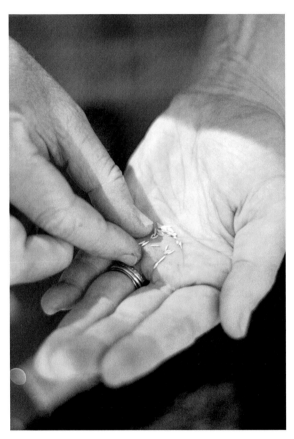

Maria and Rocco have worked on their farm in Duffys Forest most of their lives, and in fact still work the land in Duffys Forest, some 55 years after their family's first stall.

Back then, the produce grown on the farm was harvested by the family, and brought up to the roadside market stall by wheelbarrows pushed up by the kids, and displayed for sale to the public. People would travel from miles to obtain the fresh farm produce and often make a weekend trip of it.

The Italian men would go to work during the day, usually assigned to some kind of construction site and then come home to tend to the farm. During the day, the wife/mother would be working the land.

The family's market stall grew in size and became the most successful Italian market garden stall in Sydney.

The family were offered a considerable amount of money during the 1980s but declined the offer. The business was handed to Rocco's sons to continue the legacy and success, but unfortunately, as the big chain supermarkets started trading fresh produce, along with extending their trading hours from five days to seven days a week, their business experienced a rapid decline in customers.

After many years of financial security, the new market gardener generation spent more in costs than they had in profits. Sadly, the decimated business was sold.

One of the area's original Italian Migrants, selling his home-grown garden produce in his Mona Vale Road stall in the 1950s.

The site where Rocco and Maria's original tin shed stall was situated is now known as Forestway Fresh. The site was acquired by Domenic and his sons in 2006, after the collapse of the original business.

The current owner took a punt on the site, not really knowing if the collapse of the business was due to the location, new competition or just bad luck. The gamble paid off, and Forestway Fresh now successfully trades as an exceptional fresh produce store, maintaining its Italian heritage.

NEW LIFE: Incoming fruit barn operators Tony (left) and Pat Polistina.   Picture: ROS CANNON

Landmark fruit barn to reopen

SANDRA GIBSON

THE reopening of a fruit barn at Terrey Hills is the first step towards developing a neighbourhood shopping centre which could possibly include an Aldi supermarket, co-owner Domenic Polistina said yesterday.

The new Forest Way Fresh Fruit Barn, at Mona Vale and Myoora Rds, officially opens today after months lying vacant.

The landmark site, which boasts about 40 years as a fruit market, has been earmarked for numerous developments over time but none eventuated until the Polistina family bought it recently.

"We bought a corpse and now we are breathing life back into it," Mr Polistina said.

PAST, PRESENT AND FUTURE

■ **CLOSED:** The Forest Way Fruit Barn closed months ago after 40 years

■ **OPEN:** The new Forest Way Fresh Fruit Barn opens today at Mona Vale and Myoora Rds, Terrey Hills

■ **BIG PLANS:** The new owners have plans to develop a village atmosphere, with restaurants and a supermarket

Joined in the business by his brother Sam and two sons Pat and Tony, Mr Polistina said negotiations were under way to try and attract the Aldi supermarket chain to the site.

He said Aldi was "very interested" in establishing a second store on the northern beaches.

An Aldi spokeswoman would neither confirm nor deny Mr Polistina's claims yesterday, simply saying "no comment".

Mr Polistina said the family vision was to incorporate Aldi with a few restaurants, eateries and other stores to create a village-type atmosphere.

"We want to work together with the local community . . . we will be looking to develop it within the guidelines of the council to allow a permissible use of that corner."

Terrey Hills Progress Association president Frank Beckman said the re-opening of a fruit market at the site was positive for the community.

"When it closed it left the community without that extra choice and a greater variety of produce," Mr Beckman said.

"It will attract people to our area and it will cater for local residents."

Mr Beckman said there had been a proposal to develop the site into a commercial venture incorporating shops, restaurants and a neighbouring service station to which the progress association had objected.

He said the application was refused by the council and the Land and Environment Court for reasons including an insufficient sewerage system.

Warringah Council was unable to confirm yesterday that an application had been refused.

Duffys Forest still remains strong in its farming – from producing vegetables, eggs, and honey – to the local Christmas Tree Farm that sees hundreds of visitors purchasing trees to take home and decorate during the Christmas period.

The café serves some of the best coffee in Sydney.

After the Italian and Greek migration through the government's scheme, espresso coffee machines were introduced to Australia. The first machine was installed in 1928 in Melbourne but the culture soon found its way to Sydney.

The Northern Beaches has continued its legacy of sharing a beautifully made espresso coffee in numerous cafes.

Bush Lemon Jam Recipe

This bush lemon jam has quite a different flavour from the usual marmalade. The recipe was contributed to The Courier-Mail in 1945 by Mrs G. Jeffs of Kingaroy.

Slice three bush lemons finely and put on to boil with eight cups of water. Boil for 80 minutes quickly and add eight cups of sugar. Boil for 1 hour longer and bottle while still hot. The Courier-Mail (Brisbane, Qld. June 9, 1945)

The Kitchen Garden at The Farmhouse is tended to daily and produces an abundance of organic greens.

Bush Tucker

Food, typically uncooked, from plants and animals native to the Australian outback.

Until the area was colonised, food was sourced from the bush. Kangaroo, goanna, emu, crocodile, snakes, Witchetty grubs, and plants, were all on the menu. The local Guringay tribe lived on a diet rich in fish and shellfish living in such close proximity to the water. They would fish the seas and work the land for 4-5 hours per day to ensure they were well-nourished and allow for extra stock to trade between other tribes.

The indigenous way of sourcing food and consuming meals was successfully in effect for approximately 60,000 years.

Many bush food plants were also used for medicinal purposes.

The indigenous Australians believed in a holistic method of treating ailments and illness, incorporating the four dimensions being spiritual, physical, intellectual and emotional.

Source: Provenance Growers

Once the European settlers began to claim the land as theirs, bush tucker became threatened. The Aboriginal people were separated from their tribal communities, children were stolen, and their homes within the land and next to seas were destroyed, which had a profound effect on how the land and seas were managed in terms of food production and consumption. This damage has never been reversed.

Rations, with no real nutritional value such as flour and sugar, were supplied to the natives to supplement the very small amount of bush tucker now available to them. The areas became more populated, and land for hunting and gathering became redundant.

As the generations changed, tradition and learned experience working with the land and sea, with cooking with traditional methods, deteriorated. Many of the Indigenous women now worked as home-helpers for the Europeans and were learning new recipes to cook such as scones, and cakes. The newfound skills in the kitchen were introduced in their own homes, replacing the nutrient dense bush tucker once provided for their families.

However, indigenous produce was somewhat incorporated into European households by means of the need to adapt their English recipes with the indigenous ingredients on hand. One of the most popular dishes in the 1800's was a little dish called the "Kangaroo Steamer." Another couple of examples of combining the traditional English recipe with the indigenous ingredients available were Wonga Wonga Pigeon (a variation on a roasted pheasant), and Plum Pudding made with Davidson Plum.

In recent times, a trend has resurfaced in using indigenous bush foods within a modern food experience. The late 1970's/early 1980's saw an excitement in the release of cookbooks, and television shows highlighting how to use bush tucker in recipes. Today, the products are gaining even more cutting-edge attention, with real commercial value. You are able to purchase beautifully packaged indigenous foods, such as Lemon Myrtle, Davidson Plum, Teas, Pepperberries, Wattleseed, Kangaroo, Emu and the like. Exporting these goods has become a lucrative exercise.

Foods still readily available within the Gurigay peoples land (Ku Ring Gai National Park) are figs, bush tomatoes, and shellfish to name a few. I have even seen a freshwater yabbie crossing the road in our area recently! There are a few wonderful guided bush tucker tours you can book into for the day to learn what the area once looked like in terms of food, and this lost appreciation and tradition.

The Formal Dining Room at The Farmhouse

Did you know the Aboriginal Australians used to detect honey hives by pressing their ears up to a hollow tree to see if they could hear a bees' hum?

The Sugar Bag bees would build a beautiful nest for them to scoop out with an axe. The honey was extracted with a long stick with bundled grass attached to the end which resembled a mop.

Bush Tomato Soup Recipe

Ingredients

1 tablespoon olive oil
1 onion, chopped
1 clove garlic, crushed
2 tablespoons ground bush tomato
4 rashers smoked bacon, finely diced
10 ripe tomatoes, chopped
1 cup chicken or vegetable stock
salt and freshly ground black pepper natural yoghurt, to serve
chopped chives, to serve
Parmesan crisps
olive oil spray
80 g grated parmesan
Ground bush tomato, for sprinkling

Method

Heat the oil in a large saucepan and sauté the onion and garlic until softened.

Add the bush tomato, bacon, chopped tomato and sugar and simmer gently for about 30 minutes.

The tomatoes will break down and release their liquid.

Meanwhile, make the crisps.

Preheat the grill to hot.

Line a baking tray with baking paper and spray lightly with olive oil spray.

Divide the grated Parmesan into eight portions and place in little piles on the prepared tray, leaving room for spreading.

Sprinkle a small amount of bush tomato over each pile, then place under the grill and cook until the parmesan spreads to a flat disk and cooks to a rich golden colour.

Remove from oven and leave crisps to cool completely before carefully removing from the tray.

Add the stock to the soup and bring back to the boil.

Season with salt and pepper.

Using a hand-held blender, puree the soup until the tomato skins have been incorporated.

Ladle the hot soup into bowls and garnish with a dollop of yoghurt and a sprinkling of chives.

Serve the parmesan crisps on the side.

1 tablespoon olive oil
1 onion, chopped
1 clove garlic, crushed
2 tablespoons ground bush tomato
4 rashers smoked bacon, finely diced
10 ripe tomatoes, chopped

1 cup chicken or vegetable stock
salt and freshly ground black pepper
natural yoghurt, to serve
chopped chives, to serve
Parmesan crisps
olive oil spray
80 g grated parmesan
ground bush tomato, for sprinkling

Freshwater

The waterways surrounding The Farmhouse consist of freshwater bodies and distributaries. But unfortunately, these waterways are labelled endangered ecological communities.

Turtles have been around since the dinosaur times and are excellent survivors but with urban development and the increased rate of waste being deposited into the waterways – such as detergents, stormwater pollution, insecticides and chemicals – the local wildlife is endangered and so too the natural lifecycle within these habitats. This damage is threatening continuation of the flora and fauna within these areas.

When we first moved to the area, whilst driving in and out of the suburb one day, I was taken aback to spot a turtle sat in the middle of the road! We swiftly placed it to the side, to safety. Then further along, we spotted a crayfish crossing! I immediately contacted the rest of my family to notify them of the bizarre encounters, only to endure their mocking, all of them thinking I had really lost it! Little did we know that these were just two kinds of freshwater species that were native to the area.

The turtle we often see on the roads in our locale are Eastern Long Neck Turtles (My family have witnessed first-hand these gorgeous little creatures and no longer think I am insane). The turtles are one of seven freshwater species turtles found in New South Wales.

The Eastern Long Neck Turtle live for approximately fifty years. They spend most of their time in the water, however they come to land to nest. They dig a hole in the earth and lay their eggs. Once the eggs are covered with soil, the turtle eggs are left for a few months to incubate. Once the baby turtles have hatched, they make their way back into the waterways.

Unfortunately, the eggs and the infant turtles are prey to foxes, fish and even the common pet dog. There is also a high incident of road accidents with the turtles crossing the roads, unaware of the danger.

The local fresh water ways are home to two species of crayfish. The first is the less prevalent Spiny Crayfish, and the other, the humble Yabby. We were witness to the latter crossing the road on that opportune day.

Aboriginal shell midden © Margo Laidley-Scott

The Yabby is incredibly resilient. It is often referred to as "the destructor", as they are able to burrow deeply into riverbed walls causing weakness in the natural construction. They are also carnivores.

It is evident the Aboriginal people had a strong connection with the land they inhabited. The philosophy was: the land possessed them, not the other way around. The aboriginal people are said to have known every nook and cranny of their natural environments, including weather patterns, characteristics of animals and any slight change in the air which could indicate varying temperaments in their environment.

The clans inhabiting these shores from early Australian times used fishing as a primary source of nutrition. Women were actually the ones associated with fishing, with their hooks made from the inside of shells, resembling mother-of-pearl. This acted as a lure, with the attached piece of chewed up shellfish as bait. It is said the women would often sing as they fished in hope that the fish would be lured onto the line with their song.

Fishing lines were made of twisted bark and leaves while canoes were often made of bark to assist with the fishing success. Sometimes small fires were lit inside the canoes, upon seaweed or a block of clay, to enable the caught fish to be cooked immediately and enjoyed on the spot!

The preserved and protected rock engravings within the area sometimes focus on the fish life of the area. That, along with the discovery of several middens (concentrations of discarded shells, bone and ash), reinforce the importance of the freshwater sources.

Unfortunately, the middens were also a guide to the European settler in terms of where to successfully situate themselves which led to many early Australians being run out of their own land parcels.

Bees and Beekeeping

Even though Australia's bees are, for the most part, protected there is a serious threat to our beautiful bee population from human activity. Excessive land clearing in Australia, for rural farming and housing, means that many trees are being demolished that house our local bees, including our native Sugarbag Bee and their hives.

The Sugarbag Bee species is one of only 600 stingless species, both globally and native. Remarkably, the Sugarbag Bee is the only native stingless bee that produces honey.

The Sugarbag Bee is hunted by walking through scrubland in the Australian bush. If a Native Bee is spotted leaving the hollow of a tree, the hive is known to be inside. Once this tree hollow is found, the hive is removed carefully and acts as an abundant food source, sometimes providing an entire meal for a family of the First Nations People.

The Native Sugarbag Beehive was a highly prized acquisition; hives would sometimes be given as gift of mutual peace as well as fertility. Honey hunting has been in place for some 4,000 years in Australia.

THE STINGLESS BEEHIVE – TETRAGONULA CARBONARIA – THE ONLY STINGLESS, HONEY-PRODUCING BEE NATIVE TO THE AREA OF DUFFYS FOREST/TERREY HILLS AREA

Becoming a Beekeeper

The Ku-ring-gai Council offers a native beehive program, where you can learn about the nature of our native bees, and even foster a hive to take home to your own backyard. This helps ensure the sustainability of our native bees. The program has become so popular that they offer a "bee lottery", wherein you place your name on a list to enter a draw.

Terrey Hills houses The Northern Beaches Beekeepers Association. The association was established in 1954 and was known as The Amateur Beekeepers Association of NSW.

The association offers beginners' courses in beekeeping. The course runs over two days and is an excellent way to introduce yourself to backyard hobby beekeeping.

For the first time opening my own hive, I was lucky enough to have my local mentor, Michelle, by my side.

Lighting the Smoker.

Types of Hives

If you are thinking of setting up a small hive, you will need to choose the type of beehive you find resonates with you most and fits well with your environment. Bees love swimming pools so it's probably not the best idea to set up your hive right next to your neighbour's pool, for example!

The Langstroth Hive is the original beehive. These are probably what you are most familiar with when you see a few hive boxes stacked up in the middle of a field.

Langstroth designed the hive in 1850, fitting the parts neatly into a champagne box and was

awarded the patent in 1852. There have been moderate changes introduced throughout the years, but for the most part, the design ethic has remained. The Langstroth box hives are still a more experienced beekeeper's choice.

Top Bar Hives are a rectangular, long box hive set up on a stand. They include a frameless system, where the comb starts forming from the top of the internal bars and as the comb expands, it hangs down from these removable bars. As the bees are closely emulating nature within this hive, the Top Bar Hives are known as the most natural of the beekeepers' hives. The long, heavy harvest is one of the only downfalls.

Waree Hives, also known as the "peoples' hives", are wooden, boxed hives but with no comb framework infrastructure internally.

The bees build a natural comb and the process is very natural.

The Waree Hives cost a great deal less than the traditional Langstroth Hives.

The only real downside to these hives is when it comes to the extraction of honey, a tedious process of letting the honey drip from the comb into a vessel over time is the only way to extract without crushing the actual comb itself.

FlowHive

We are lucky enough to have the wonderful invention of FLOWHIVE in Australia designed by a clever father-and-son duo from Byron Bay. The system was advertised on a crowdfunding page and the amount of interest surpassed their wildest dreams. It raised over ten million dollars and took hundreds of pre-sale orders from all over the globe in the first year.

This is the Hive we have on the property.

Safety Gear

The next step is your safety gear.

Did you know that bees are on high alert to black clothing? It is because they still have an instilled memory of the Black Bear being a threat. I turned up to my very first day of beekeeping dressed in black from head-to-toe. Those bees marked me as a predator from the start! Learned the hard way.

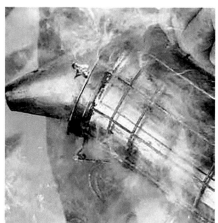

So, if you're new to this, DON'T WEAR BLACK! Light colours, preferably white, are best.

Similarly, bees aren't keen on perfume, horse sweat, bananas, wool, loud noises, thunderstorms or vibrations caused by the waving of hands around your face!

Always wear gloves.

You can purchase these from a plethora of cool beekeeping gear but your everyday rubber dishwashing gloves will also do the trick! They are easier to feel through from a tactile perspective and you are also less prone to accidently squish a poor little bee.

If you are going to use household kitchen gloves, remember not to wear black or red!

A beekeepers' jacket/suit is definitely a must. You can find these online or at your local beekeepers'.

The same goes for a smoker. The smoker is an important tool which helps you calm the bees when you are working with the hive and is very useful if you do happen to be stung. The smoke masks the venom odours expelled from a bee that has stung, warning the other bees there is a predator.

So now you have your hive, your kit, your smoker and your not-to-do's! Time for bees!

There are a few ways to encourage a colony of bees into your new hobby hive.

You can have a professional experienced beekeeper collect a swarm from a natural environment for you and bring it back to house in your own hive.

Other choices include purchasing a "package" from either an experienced beekeeper or online (but make sure you buy from a reputable beekeeper as you don't want cranky bees, trust me!) and having them delivered right to your door or acquiring a nucleus swarm or "nuc" as they are known in in the business. A "nuc" is two to three frames already well on their way to being established as a hive. The frames are placed within your hive and the process continues but your waiting time until harvest is obviously lessened.

Either way, just make sure you have a mentor with you to get you started.

Also make sure you register as a beekeeper online to be identified. This will allow you not only the cool certification, but to be informed of any outbreaks of disease in your immediate area.

I participated in a two-week course held by The Northern Beaches Amateur BeeKeepers Association. I would highly recommend this training to anyone wanting to keep bees at home.

Beeswax

Australia has the purest beeswax in the world. Our bees are not prone to the disease Varroa Mite. This disease is a problem for bees all over the world except Australia. Australian beeswax is free of pesticides, hives are not moved often and our bees have a healthy diet, which all makes for a pure wax.

Some beekeepers have switched over to harvesting the wax only and the financial reward is almost double to that of harvesting and supplying honey. Wax is used for candles, surfboard wax, food wrapping and the likes.

Candles have been a popular product of beehives for centuries, with monasteries keeping their own beehives so they could make candles independently from the comb. The candles made from the beeswax were clean burning and did not have a damaging effect on the cathedrals and monasteries' ceiling paintings. Bees were highly revered.

Did you know that during wartime, beeswax was used to coat the wings of fighter planes and bullets to make them glide faster in the air?

In New South Wales, almond farmers have a very important use for bees.

During the season, beekeepers are sourced to move their hives into the almond farms to help pollenate. The beekeepers are offered somewhere in the region of $300–400 per hive, making this proposition much more profitable than making honey.

Unfortunately, this is not ideal for the bees, as they are not in a natural environment and able to gather protein, nectar and water. So they often feel depleted.

Unless the bees are taken directly to a canola field immediately to replenish, the beehives are more often than not, lost.

THE
AMATEUR
BEEKEEPER

Registered at the G.P.O. Sydney for transmission by post as a periodical – Category B

News bulletin for The Amateur Beekeepers' Association of N.S.W.

Vol.11 No.8   Price $1.70 p.a.   August, 1974

President: Mr. Ken Parry, 68 Bruce St., Brighton-le-Sands. Ph.595772
General Secretary: Mr. Colin Mettam, 95 Waratah St., Kirrawee. 2232
General Treasurer: Mr. Cecil Luff, 559 Mowbray Rd., Lane Cove. 2066
Bulletin Editor: Mr. Milton Parry, 68 Bruce St., Brighton-le-Sands 2216

THE EFFECT OF SMOKE ON BEES

Why does smoking a colony calm the bees? Beekeepers who have observed smoked bees have noticed that the bees engorge with honey; Dr. Free, of the Rothamsted Station in England, has studied the question more extensively.

It was observed that the amount of food in the honey stomach of bees that were smoked was greater than those which were not smoked. Two hours after the bees were smoked this was still the case.

Ten minutes after a colony was smoked the bees had the greatest quantity of food in their honey stomachs. This indicates that waiting a few minutes after a colony is smoked to examine it would lessen the danger of being stung. Dr. Free also observed that guard bees, at the entrance of the colony, had the least amount of food in their honey stomachs.

However, in a colony which is smoked, only about half of the bees engorge. It is suggested that smoke may calm a colony in other ways in addition to causing the bees to feed. Smoke may cover up an objectionable scent and/or disorganize a colony.

::::::::::::::::::::::::::::::

We keep chickens at home on the property. Its rewards include no food scrap wastage and a ready supply of fresh eggs.

TERREY HILLS WOMEN'S ASSOCIATION

Object: Terrey Hills Community Centre.

Mrs. S. Cooke.

14/6/53.

Mrs. L.M.Rhodes.

Booralie Rd.,
TERREY HILLS.

The Hon. Secretary,
Aust. Red Cross Society,
TERREY HILLS BRANCH.

Dear Mrs. Coleman,

As you are aware, the overall programme of the combined associations was prepared early in the year when it was thought that the Community Hall would be available about June.

However, the tentative opening date has now been set for 12th. Sept, which means that functions which were to have been held before that date have necessarily been cancelled.

The Flower Show & Exhibition of work (including a cooking section) has been changed from 12th. to 26th Sept, and a new date will be forwarded to you as soon as available. How (...)

You might also regard that entire elections will most likely be held early in November, and in the event of this we will be conducting stalls as usual.

Another date not shown on the programme is 18th Dec, when a Xmas function is to be held in the Hall.

In the meantime we would like to invite your members to a social afternoon to be held at the home of Mrs. Tom Cooke on Thursday, 23rd. July at 2 p.m. Afternoon tea will be served for 2/-, and there will be cards, hoopla, novelty competitions, etc. Proceeds go towards the Community Centre, and all will be very welcome.

Yours sincerely,

L. Rhodes

Hon.

AUSTRALIAN RED CROSS SOCIETY

INCORPORATED BY ROYAL CHARTER 1941

NEW SOUTH WALES DIVISION

Terrey Hills BRANCH

West Head Rd.
Terrey Hills
21st. 2.53.

Dear Mrs Rhodes,

We thank you for your letter of the 12th instant re programme arrangements of our various functions for the Red Cross. Two members of our Branch will attend the Terrey Hills Women's Assn. meeting to be held at the home of Mrs Sainsbury on March 5th.

Yours sincerely,

H. Coleman

Hon. Sec.

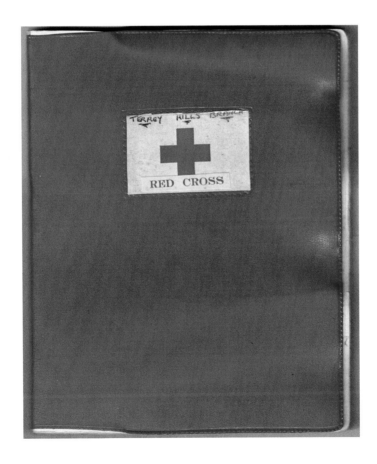

The Terrey Hills Division, Red Cross Ladies.
Doreen Bibby, Dulcie Cook, Mrs Clues, Grace Sainsbury, Pearl Field, Helen Coleman, Mrs Thistleton

During my research for this book, I found a connection to the past. As an active member of The Red Cross Society of Women Leaders myself, it was heart-warming to discover that there was a dedicated local Red Cross division in the '50s. They formed an integral part of a larger NSW branch with members of other divisions.

The Red Cross principles remain the same to this day.

RED CROSS PRINCIPLES

HUMANITY
: The Red Cross endeavours, in its international and national capacity, to prevent and alleviate human suffering wherever it may be found.

  Its purpose is to protect life and health and to ensure respect for the human being.

IMPARTIALITY
: It makes no discrimination as to nationality, race religious beliefs, class or political opinions.

NEUTRALITY
: The Red Cross may not take sides in hostilities or engage at any time in controversies of a political, racial, religious or idealogical nature.

INDEPENDENCE
: The Red Cross is independent. The National Societies must always maintain their autonomy so that they may be able at all times to act in accordance with Red Cross principles.

VOLUNTARY SERVICE
: The Red Cross is a voluntary relief organisation not prompted in any manner by desire for gain.

UNITY
: There can be only one Red Cross Society in any one country. It must be open to all. It must carry on its humanitarian work throughout its territory.

UNIVERSALITY
: The Red Cross is a world-wide institution in which all Societies have equal status and share equal responsibilities and duties in helping each other.

PRIMARY OBJECTS OF THE SOCIETY

Furnishing of aid to the sick and wounded, irrespective of nationality.

Rendering of assistance in the case of great public disaster, calamity or need.

Improvement of health.

Prevention of disease.

Mitigation of suffering in Australia and elsewhere.

Fire

Aboriginal Uses

To cook food, the local Indigenous people would make use of the ground. These ground ovens were constructed by digging a hole in the dirt. Next, a fire would be lit inside.

The fire would burn down and large stones would be placed strategically to circulate heat, just like that of a conventional oven. If cooking an animal, the skins would act as protective wrapping and would then be removed prior to eating. Another traditional method was to let the fire turn to ash and then cook food encased in leaves, buried beneath the ashes.

Even snakes were baked in the coal, with the most venomous snakes still being eaten but avoiding the glands on the head to ensure no venom was ingested. The locals were considered to be "the Saltwater People" and lived on crayfish, oysters, fish and local sea fare, in addition to food sources from the land.

Cleansing and purifying "country" with Native flora such as the Acacia tree branch, which was lit on fire and then left smoking, was an important ritual for Indigenous culture. This ceremony is called a NUMBUK YABUN. It is not dissimilar to the theory of a sage smudge stick.

Firing the grass was a good way to attract animals to hunters. Many of the bushfires over the past thousands of years had been deliberately lit. This management of the land was known as "patterning".

It consisted of the land being split into sections like a large jigsaw, using parts of it as farmable land, while other parts were burnt back to assist with renewed vegetation regrowth as well as enticing animals back for hunting. The fires also eliminated snakes.

With the growing concern about bushfires, we look back at the land management principles of the Indigenous. There is a wonderful book on this topic, called The Biggest Estate on Earth: How *Aborigines Made Australia*, by Bill Gammage. It gives a thorough account of the early land management success and the damage we have done to the land with simple arrogance and I urge you to read it!

The Outdoor Firepit at The Farmhouse

A pile burn is the burning of cut and stacked vegetation, usually during the winter when the vegetation is dry. The pile burns are the step before back burning to ensure all small dry debris has been removed to ensure a safe back burning effort.

Duffys Forest Fire Station

In 1947, the Duffys Forest Rural Fire Brigade was born. The brigade's captain transported the equipment donated by Warringah Council in his Ford flat-top truck. A few years later, a local resident donated a Chevrolet to be used as a tanker.

A shed was built soon after by volunteers, becoming the first official site of the Duffys Forest Fire Brigade. In 1965, the station was officially opened and has since remained in operation.

In the mid-1960s, a special ladies crew was established. Their role was to curtail any smaller local fires that may have started in the area before their husbands had time to travel back from work and take over the fight.

Former RFS Commissioner, Shane Fitzsimmons, started his journey right here at the Duffys Forest Fire Brigade as a volunteer when he was only fifteen years old. In his role as fire commissioner, he represented over 72,000 volunteers in the State.

Sadly, he lost his father, only 53 at the time, in a local back burning exercise that became out of control.

The Duffys Forest area has been susceptible to fires in the past, with two major bushfires in 1951, in which six homes and six lives were lost.

Shane Fitzsimmons in earlier days.
He was named Australian of the Year in 2019.

DUFFY'S FOREST BUSH FIRE BRIGADE

wish to announce their

Get-Together

at

The Fire Shed

Anembo Road, Duffy's Forest

on

Saturday, 28th February, 1976, at 6.30 p.m.

Bring: Your Family and Friends

Eating Utensils

Steak and Sausages

New South Wales Rural Fire Service

WARRINGAH-PITTWATER DISTRICT
DUFFYS FOREST BRIGADE

The members of the **Duffys Forest Rural Fire Brigade** would like you to join with us at the official opening of the new station additions.

This is to be held at the Fire Station, Anembo Rd, Duffys Forest, on **Sunday 22 April 2001**, (our 37th Birthday) commencing at **1.00 pm**.

Following the ceremony at **2.00pm**, light refreshments will be served.

To assist with catering, would you kindly RSVP by phoning the Station on 94501144.
Should no one be in attendance, please leave a message.

OLD-FASHIONED bucket brigade methods save a caravan in McCarrs Creek Road, Terrey Hills.   *Picture: GLENN DIPLEY*

Newspaper clipping and original correspondence collected from the Terrey Hills Public library archives.

Duffys Forest Rural Fire Brigade
Anembo Road
Duffys Forest 2084
PO Box 328 Terrey Hills, 2084
Telephone: 9450-1144
Facsimile: 9450-1372

Duffys Forest Rural Fire Brigade

Gun Club

The New South Wales Gun Club is the oldest gun club in Australia, established in 1880 and originally located in Mascot on the site which is the new Sydney Domestic Airport.

In 1946, a parcel of land in Terrey Hills was acquired and the club was relocated. Joining fees were the equivalent of $3,000 per annum in today's currency.

The club is historically noted as being one of the oldest licensed establishments in NSW. Celebrating 140 years, there are now over 500 members, with visitors added each year, who practise, compete and socialise at the club.

Sir Robert Lucas-Tooth Founder, NSW Gun Club

Wood Fired Oven

When designing the interiors of the farmhouse, a reference to the Italian "Masseria" (Italian for farmhouse) was included. One of the items included in the kitchen build was a traditional wood-fired oven.

The wood-fired oven is used not only for pizzas, but slow-cooking meats and vegetables, along with breakfast skillets of bacon and eggs. It also acts as a heater for the kitchen area during the cooler months.

Wood-fired ovens date back as early as the sixteenth century and were mostly used for baking bread.

The addition of the pizza oven to the kitchen gives the space authenticity to the Italian way, and a space to create with food, on a very earthy level.

Fillies and Friends

The first horses to arrive in Australia came over on the First Fleet along with the first female convicts. It's believed that one stallion, three mares and three colts were on board. By the nineteenth century, better blood-lined fillies were brought in and the thoroughbred lineage is still traceable to this day.

Encounters between Early Australians and the European settlers were often on horseback. Initially, the indigenous people, used to being on foot, feared the animal, frightened of being bitten; comparing a horse to that of a larger domesticated dog.

Once our Early Australians learned the relationship between man and horse, they then pursued taming and training the horses on the plains of red dust in the outback. This enabled them to become mountain trackers.

Unfortunately, many of the clashes and massacres at the time had parties meet each other, riding in the saddle.

One of the first roads on the Northern Beaches connected Cowan Creek to what we know today as Mona Vale Road. It was originally a rough bush track used by the inhabitants. Mona Vale Road was later established after many watched how the timber getters of Duffys Forest used these pathways for bullock transportation of lumber and firewood, along with flowers cut by the wives that were then taken to the nearest village of St Ives for sale.

This road was travelled upon extensively by men on horseback during the 1800s, often carting fruit produced from orchards in the area, among one reason for expeditions.

Pony Clubs

The families of Terrey Hills/Duffys Forest have long held riding lessons, albeit these days more a hobby than a skill required out of necessity. The first pony club proper was established in 1986. The Terrey Hills Riding School is owned and operated by a very accomplished local, Lauren Seeley. Lauren migrated to Australia from Canada in 2004 and found work using her formal qualifications as an IVF genetic scientist. For over 10 years, Lauren worked as a scientist in the city while balancing her love and passion for horses by riding and training as an obsessive hobby in her spare time. In 2017, Lauren quit her job as a scientist to work with horses full-time, coaching, teaching lessons, and training and riding her own and client horses. For Lauren, the best part about giving up the 'city job' to work with horses and riders full time is spending each and every day outdoors, doing something she loves, and sharing that passion and the joy of the horses with others who feel the same. Lauren currently competes at 2* level eventing, elementary dressage, and 1.20m show jumping with the ambition and aspiration to train and compete at higher world-class levels.

Amazingly, there are over 500 horses stabled in the Terrey Hills/Duffys Forest area, about as many as people!

The original club room still stands today within the grounds of The NSW Gun Club. The club house was also utilised as a library and at times by The Australian Red Cross.

The club was named Forest Hill Pony Club, combining one part of both Duffys Forest and Terrey Hills in unison.

In 1991, a terrible storm caused havoc, with large fallen trees destroying much of the riding clubs' facilities and the club was forced to relocate. During subsequent years, to gain access to the new site meant having to cross Mona Vale Road. This was a treacherous ride and a dangerous crossing due to four-lane traffic.

Police escorts were temporarily implemented to allow for safe crossings. Locals made a plea to the government to upgrade the roads, including an underpass, and this was successful, allowing safer and easier travel to the new site. The Terrey Hills-based Pony Club still remains today, successful in its intentions.

Several riding schools opened in the years following, around the Terrey Hills/Duffys Forest area, including The Terrey Hills Riding School, established in 1986.

The area is heavily populated with horseback riders meandering to and from the various trails, plus to and from the public arena situated at Anembo Reserve, which was upgraded and re-opened in 2011 for trail use.

Sally supplies locals with farm fresh eggs, homemade jams and honey. She adores her plethora of pets!

Fetch

Canines form a significant part of Indigenous Australian life and mythology, firstly with the dingo and later with the domestic dog. The relationship between canines and Indigenous Australians is unique in that these peoples never domesticated the wild dingo.

Apart from featuring in Indigenous Australian spirituality, camp dingoes and dogs were protectors, bed warmers and companions. However, the downsides included potential disruption to camp life and ceremonies, one more burden on camp food supplies and perhaps a source of disease.

Researchers believe the Dingo was introduced by Indonesian travellers some thousands of years ago. Far from being simply a pest, some propose that Dingoes can help to restore some of our degraded rangelands, although research is still ongoing.

The domestic dog was introduced to Australia by the explorers and settlers of the 1700s.

The blood-sport of dog and cock fights were a common occurrence during these times and this infiltrated the community of Duffys Forest. These illegal practices went unnoticed by the authorities as the events took place in the deep forested areas of Terrey Hills and Duffys Forest and were often alcohol-fuelled with smuggled-in rum and other spirits.

With land parcels in the area still measured in acres rather than metres, the area has become a natural location for Dog Boarding Houses. The area is peppered with kennels providing care for pets whilst owners holiday abroad. Today we Aussies are magnificent dog lovers with just under half of the population owning a pet dog.

We own a beautiful Hungarian Vizsla called Daisy May. She often plays chase with two Plover birds she has connected with and mimics our resident Wallabies by bouncing around the property.

Skippy

Our original farmhouse was built during the time an Australian television series was being filmed in the area, that was later to become an Australian Icon.

If you are an Australian child of the '70s, chances are you grew up with a very clever Kangaroo called Skippy The Bush Kangaroo. The show aired from 1967 until 1969 but repeated for years afterwards.

In the late 1960s, Kerry Packer (owner of Channel 9) was granted permission by the New South Wales Government to use a 24-acre parcel of Crown Land as a film set for the filming of this now "National Treasure".

Within the Ku-Ring-Gai Chase National Park, sits the fictional Waratah Park, once the home of Skippy's friends, along with the beautiful and very real parcel of land called Duffys Forest.

Because of its pop culture heritage, Waratah Park operated as a very successful tourist attraction until 2006.

Waratah Park, once Crown Land, was handed to the Metropolitan Aboriginal Local Land Council in 2014. The council received $10,000 to begin the restoration of Waratah Park. These funds will be used to draw up the initial plans of restoring the site back to its original splendour.

Works are now underway to utilise the site as an area for education. The restored Waratah Park, along with a separate Aboriginal Cultural Centre, will share the same site. The intention is to connect the Aboriginal community back to the site, along with continuing the legacy of the iconic TV series, Skippy the Bush Kangaroo.

This poster is an old image of all types of kangaroos and was found on site by the photographer.

Decades on, this is the set bedroom for Sonny on the show.

A location within Duffys Forest where the show was filmed for some years

Waratah Park: home of the cuddly koala

magic of animals
by Garry Somerville

Australia's unique flora and fauna in all its splendor is right at your doorstep in Waratah Park at Duffys Forest.

Since the bushfires of 1979-80 a change has occurred and emphasis has now been placed on the park's zoological significance and its identity as the home of Skippy, our internationally famous kangaroo.

One of the key attractions is the display and breeding of koalas.

Koala is an aboriginal word meaning "no drink." Do you know why?

Unlike kangaroos, koalas don't drink. They rely on the moisture content of leaf fodder.

If they are seen drinking it often indicates ill health.

Their diet, even today, is a bit of a mystery, but we do know they mostly feed on certain species of eucalyptus.

Visitors under the supervision of expert staff, can observe, photograph and touch these unique and delightful animals.

They are not nearly as unpleasant as the Federal Minister for Tourism, Mr Brown, would have us believe.

A few years ago koalas were on the "vanishing list" but management programs like Waratah Park have slowly reversed the situation.

Today they are increasing in numbers.

A spokesman for the park told me: "Bringing native animals, birds and people close together in a lovely Australian bush setting is what Waratah Park is all about."

Walk-in enclosures enable visitors to mingle with kangaroos (often with joeys in the pouch) and hand feed emus.

Then there are the wombats, dingos, Tasmanian devils, wallabies and cockatoos.

Covering 40 acres it has bush walks and a unique bush railway travels a scenic route through bushland adjacent to Ku-ring-gai Chase National Park.

Anyone living in the Peninsula area may not be aware that Waratah Park managing director Naish Hogan provides a free advisory service for koala lovers.

Naish will advise what species of eucalyptus to plant which will attract koalas and where to get them.

With still some koalas living and breeding in the area it is important for them to maintain their survival residency.

While talking to Naish I gained the impression he was a man who has dedicated his life to improve the lives and welfare of our delightful koalas.

Three young koalas from Waratah [...] bottom) Matilda, Jessica an[...]

Waratah Park up for heritage decision

D-DAY ON SKIPPY'S HOME

Brenton Cherry

STORY SO FAR

- Filming of Skippy commenced in 1967 at Waratah Park and wound up in 1969 after 91 episodes.
- The set was then opened to the public in 1970 as a theme park and animal sanctuary.
- In 2003 it was taken over by Earth Sanctuaries which had plans to enhance the native flora and fauna.
- The parent company, however, failed in 2006 and the park was closed with all semi-tame kangaroos and wallabies removed in 2009.
- In 2011 Warringah Council nominated Waratah Park for heritage listing.

WARATAH Park could soon be protected with the State Heritage Register Committee to consider its official listing.

The future of the home of Skippy the Bush Kangaroo has been uncertain ever since it closed as a wildlife park in 2006.

Over the years a number of developers have tried to buy the 12ha site, which has also been subject to a land claim by the Metropolitan Local Aboriginal Land Council.

Last year Warringah Council nominated Waratah Park for inclusion on the State Heritage Register in a bid to prevent it being privately acquired and carved up.

Now the Heritage Branch has completed its report on the proposal, which was formally put to the committee and will be considered soon.

watching the Skippy series and become attached to this image of the Australian bushland."

The staff said the site is at risk as it has no current heritage protection and "could be sold to a developer who may wish to demolish [...]"

Skippy's protector

by SANDRA GIBSON

SKIPPING to the chase, Opposition Leader John Brogden has promised to protect Waratah Park at Terrey Hills from future development by slapping a heritage order on the site.

This is despite the State Government's assurance that any application to rezone and develop the park would be rejected.

Last Saturday Mr Brogden took his election campaign to the home of Skippy the bush kangaroo, announcing plans to save the 12ha site.

Waratah Park is famous for being the location for filming of the Skippy program, which at its peak was screened in 80 countries.

Recently the park's operator, Naish Hogan, who has run Waratah Park since the late 1970s, sought expressions of interest for its future use.

In an attempt to ensure the park's protection, the Coalition plans to place an interim heritage order immediately on the "ranger headquarters" and other buildings used in the production of the series.

This would be followed by a ministerial recommendation to the Heritage Council for a permanent heritage order.

Election vow . . . John Brogden promises to protect the home of Skippy the bush kangaroo   Picture: JOE MURPHY

Fables and Fenders

The very first musical instrument played in Australia was the didgeridoo. Its origin is said to date back over 50,000 years.

With the European culture spreading throughout Australia from the early 1700s, the songs often sung by boatloads of convicts from the British Isles introduced folk music to the land. The traditional folklore music passed on to us can still be heard in popular ballads, such as Click Go the Shears and Waltzing Matilda.

Early musicians cleverly combined the lyrics and tunes of folk music imported from the English, Europeans and Americans and then played on native Aboriginal instruments. The sound became our own.

After the war, the Australian folklore ballads were written about hardships of the time.

This continued right into the 1980s, with a new wave of music called Australian Folk Rock. One of the most memorable songs from the era was *I was only Nineteen*, by Redgum in 1983, an anti-war song.

Rock and Roll became popular in Australia with several waves of inspired rock music.

The Northern Beaches seems to be a place of intense rock talent within the modern music world, with bands such as INXS and ANGUS AND JULIA STONE starting their careers as kids living in "The Beaches".

Nowadays, chart toppers such as FLUME, OCEAN ALLEY, LIME CORDIAL, and our very own PINKISCOOL also take centre stage (quite literally!) when it comes to Northern Beaches internationally acclaimed modern musical talent.

Local Brass Band

The Warringah Concert Brass Band was established in Terrey Hills on January 1, 1979. The band is a collective of the Warringah Concert Band and the Warringah Community Brass Band consisting of sixty members in total. The group was formed by a Terrey Hills Public School teacher, Jack Saunders, with the majority of band members being students from the school.

Once the members from this predominantly school-based band had finished their primary education and moved on, Jack realised there were no other avenues for him to play in a community ensemble. From here, the band originally named the Terrey Hills District Brass Band, was born.

By 1986, there were enough band members to compete professionally. They came second place in their very first competition and have not looked back since, with a plethora of awards to date.

In 1999, Jack's son, John, took over as director of the band, continuing the legacy. 2019 celebrated the band's fortieth year together.

The Warringah Concert Band has been an integral community supporter. Every year since 1980, during the month of October, the band joins the local church in a non-denominational gathering with a salvation army officer leading the congregation.

October marks the start of the bushfire season here. The band plays for the local firefighters before they head out for their service to the community as a kind of blessing to the fleet of fire trucks. It is an incredibly moving traditional service, reflect on the role the rural fire service pay to prevent loss of life and property.

In the '60s, Englishman and Big Band enthusiast, Eric Jupp, was employed by the ABC to compose a TV show called The Magic of Music. He hit the right note and EMI signed him to produce multiple albums called Magic of Music, right into the mid-1970s.

Eric Jupp is probably most well-known for his composition of the intro music to the television series "Skippy the Bush Kangaroo". The lyrics that accompanied the composition was written by Ted Roberts.

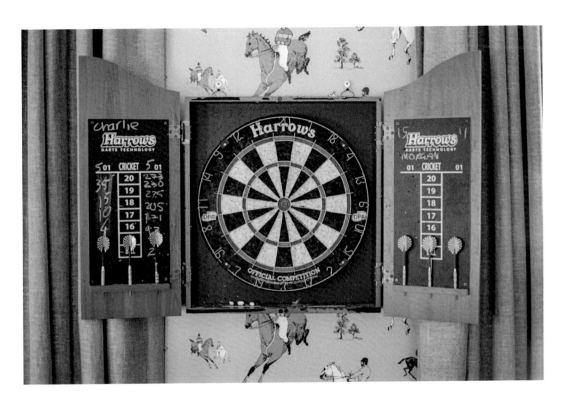

The wallpaper had definitely seen better days before the dartboard was hung in its place! The perforations are a beautiful reminder of happy and healthy competition.

The library in The Farmhouse is a special place to tuck yourself away. The walls are lined with books and the open fire creates a beautiful ambience.

This library has seen the boys through their exam studies, along with acting as a home-office meeting space and even an intimate candlelit dining area for special dinners.

Sunshine, succulents and spinning vinyls.

Music fills The Farmhouse daily. The Ukulele was handmade for the music room and engraved with a gold letter "R" representing the name of the farmhouse, over a horseshoe.

The British colonisation brought with it stern discouragement towards the First Nation people partaking in traditional games and recreations. Rather, they were persuaded to play the sports with what they named "white values", such as cricket, as a way of assimilating aboriginals into the new culture.

Along with the popular game of cricket, traditional European competitive sports and other pastimes, such as football, hunting and horseracing were introduced. Adding to that, they brought town fairs and family picnics to the list of activities for enjoyment.

The Pittwater became the playground to the wealthy, with newly formed transport methods in place inviting picnickers and campers. Excursions on steamers opened up the waterways around the area.

These recreational picnic days were often held on large parcels of acreage on the outskirts of the city, owned by wealthy landlords. Terrey Hill and Duffys Forest were among these locations.

Apple cider was hand pressed by locals to add to the picnic fare.

Rum smugglers were also apparent during these times bringing in wooden crates full of bottles of rum to the wharf at Cowan Creek. These were sometimes shipped in all the way from Indonesia.

Continuing the European traditions introduced to Australia, in 1950, the Terrey Hills Cricket Club was formed.

A second team, named the Cooyong cricket team, established themselves in 1960, but did not gain the following required to play.

A gentleman by the name of Michael Ryan reformed the Cooyong team in 1965. He and his brother coached both teams into successful competition with some of the boys' teams still competing to this day within the Manly-Warringah district.

Combining the youth and the men's teams, over 25 premierships have been won throughout the history of the Terrey Hills Cricket Club.

In 1973, the "Vikings" were formed: being the first soccer team for Terrey Hills. Competing in their black and white get-up were four teams (two youth teams and two adult teams) within the Manly-Warringah matches.

In 1986, the Vikings merged with the Belrose team, The Raiders. The team is now known as The Belrose Terrey Hills Raiders and is a large club, with divisions in nearly every age group, from under 6's right up to senior teams.

The local Rugby Union team has been celebrated over the years.

The first Union team was pulled together in 1966 by two local families. The intention was for the club to appeal to the younger players of the area forming a Junior Club team. This was a plot to decrease the driving time for parents to and from training and games from the closest club at the time, St Ives.

The original kit (sky blue and white) looks incredibly similar to our current NSW State side stripe, but the Mighty Wolves added a change, with a stronger blue- and-white vertical stripe.

Some of the original players still don this uniform and compete in the Golden Oldies matches, with the team name "The Stillbillies". These friendly games attract ex-world class rugby union players from all over the globe.

Rugby League was not as popular within the area. The initial team was formed in 1977 but unfortunately folded due to lack of local enthusiasm.

Terrey Hills Golf and Country Club

In the early '90s, Terrey Hills opened Sydney's premier golf club, Terrey Hills Golf and Country Club. The city had not seen a refurbished or newly built golf club in over twenty years. The build cost in the vicinity of $100 million, mostly due to the extensive preparation required, as the original site was an old quarry.

The newly opened course attracted some of Sydney's most elite.

Membership now stands at around 750, with some impressive names on the list. The club has hosted a myriad of competitions, but most notably the Australian Women's Open, in 2003.

Mountain biking has become popular in the area with trails ranging from 7km to 30km. Some of the trails are named The Perimeter, Cowan, Cullamine, Sandy Wilkins Loop, Neverfail and Long Trails.

These trails are naturally beautiful, with abundant native flora and fauna, waterfalls and a beautiful showcase of rich aboriginal culture and legacy. Rock engravings and evidence of original tribal sites/burial sites are still in existence. Some 350 rock engravings have been recorded in the area to this day but it is said there are many more yet to be discovered.

Community Stories

PIP SMITH

Company Director for Dick Smith Electronics

Born in 1949, Pip previously lived in Avalon and then Greenwich with her family, consisting of her husband, and two daughters Hayley, and Jenny.

Pip has lived in the area since 1979 with her husband, Dick Smith, initially buying a block of land with a fibro cottage situated on it. They built a brick home on the site and moved into their new abode on July 4, 1980, with their daughters. Pip fell in love with the area's acreage proposition and space.

With her husband's purchase of a helicopter, some land was required where he could keep his helicopter, along with flying in and out.

After searching for property within Terrey Hills, the opportunity to purchase the aforementioned land, situated on the border of Ku-Ring-Gai National Park, presented itself and allowed for Dick to be able to fly in and out without disturbing the neighbours.

Both Pip and her husband Dick have been integral community members, supporting the Terrey Hills Public School (where daughters Hayley and Jenny attended), The Terrey Hills Library and the local bushfire brigade. They also built The Australian

Pip (holding an orphaned wallaby; the family a National Parks permit to hand rear), Hayley (aged nine years), Jenny (aged seven years) and Dick.

Geographic Centre in 1986 which served as the headquarters of the publication Australian Geographic (originally entitled Dick Smith's Australian Geographic). This was subsequently sold to Fairfax Media in 1995.

When asking Pip how she feels about the area's growth, her response was, 'Actually I do not want any more "growth" in the area. I love the space, the bush, homes with gardens and the rural environment, surrounded by our beautiful Australian bush.'

With one of the biggest changes in the Terrey Hills area being the development of a retirement village near the town centre, with more development looming, Pip fears the rural aspect will eventually disappear, bringing increased traffic and loss of wildlife. But for now, Pip enjoys the area's peacefulness of this small community along with the proximity to the Northern Beaches and the City.

THELMA Florence Cook HILLS

BORN NOVEMBER 6 1923 - PASSED DECEMBER 2021

In 1881, Thelma's grandfather Samuel Hills, along with Obediah James Terrey, purchased a large parcel of land to graze sheep. James bought 640 acres and Samuel 100 acres. Both built homes on their farming land.

Elizabeth Hills

The area became known as Terrey Hills from 1934.

The Hills Children

The Hills had eight children, the third being Joseph John, born in 1867. Joseph John (or JJ as he was known) was the eldest son. JJ was one of the first wildflower and fern distributors in the area.

In 1907, JJ started a viable business, picking wildflowers and ferns from the area of Terrey Hills and transporting them, often by foot, to the city markets to sell. Since the business grew, JJ was able to hire a truck from which to sell his flowers from once a week. The business grew in success and a ten-acre block was purchased on The Mona Vale Road, on the Terrey Hills side.

This land was used to grow flowers commercially by the Hill family. The family ran the business with an entirely "hands on" approach and the children picked flowers very early in the morning before getting ready for school.

During this time, JJ married his second wife, Elizabeth. Elizabeth went on to have seven Hills children, three boys, and four girls. Thelma sits right in the middle of them all.

She describes her childhood as very strict, with her days filled with working in the fields picking wildflowers, milking the cows, collecting eggs and the like. Sadly, her childhood does not evoke many happy memories and she was in year 4 before she attended school.

Even though Terrey Hills Public School had opened, JJ refused to allow his children to attend a "common" school and so he made arrangements for them to attend St Ives Public School. Each day, a gentleman by the name of Mr Travis would gather up "The Hillbillies" as the Hills children were fondly named, and children of the Curry family, and transport them all by bus to school.

During a tumultuous time, Elizabeth decided to part ways with JJ, taking her four daughters with her to reside elsewhere. The boys stayed with JJ to work.

Meanwhile, Thelma was able to expand her skills and started working as a pastry chef in Turramurra at The Wattle Bakery. With no experience in the trade, she had to learn the skill very quickly becoming more then apt within her field.

Furthering her qualifications, Thelma taught at the Waitara Dance School as a ballroom dance teacher. Whilst teaching there, she met Sam Wood, also a dance instructor at the school.

Thelma was nineteen years old when she and Sam met. Soon after, he was conscripted to war. He proposed marriage to Thelma before they parted ways, not knowing if they would see each other again. Sam would be posted to New Guinea for the next five years. Upon his return, they were married at The Turramurra Methodist Church in 1945. Thelma was 23 years old.

She describes her marriage as a very happy unity with a beautiful home environment and happy holidays in their beach house in Newport, spilling out with children/grandchildren and food in abundance. With Sam now working as a qualified butcher, and with her mastered skills as a pastry chef, the holiday house food was always a highlight for all.

Thelma spent hours in the kitchen preparing meals for the family on these holidays, while the children were scooped up by the older women of the family and taken out to the beach for the day. Apparently, Thelma's scones were something else!

When Thelma was twenty-five, she had one son, Gary, together with Sam and after a hysterectomy at an early age, another son by way of adoption.

During Thelma's time as a homemaker in the 1940s and 1950s, she became an integral community member, volunteering at The Red Cross shop in Newport and becoming an active golfer. She very proudly stated that she still had the long-service medals at home, celebrating over thirty years of service to The Red Cross, and that she played many golf tournaments for both Asquith and Palm Beach clubs.

Thelma only recently ceased her golfing games due to her age and no longer being able to drive.

She spent her time at home, or with her sons' family, on outings. A family lunch occurred every weekend which Thelma looked forward to. Present at the family lunches were her son, and her daughter-in-law, Chris, who she shared a uniquely close relationship with.

When I asked Chris what her most poignant lesson learnt from Thelma was, she replied, 'Thelma has always been so loving and caring. It is the reason I am grateful and compassionate. She taught me to be wholeheartedly grateful for what you have and to not feel cheated for what you do not have.'

Having lived through a tough working childhood, a family separation at a young age, war, the option of having more biological children taken away from her and many more hardships, Thelma has beaten all odds and made the choice to carry herself with only positive forward-thinking drive. She is somewhat like her own mother, a woman of superlative substance, with a pure and kind spirit, and a soft, gentle heart full of soul.

Thelma has successfully instilled strong morals and ethics within her family, especially when it comes to the women lineage. She is proud of the girls and when asked what would be the most important legacy to leave behind for them, she answered, 'That they stay the same.'

JJ was described as a very hard man with extreme masculine views. Joseph John died of diabetes that was left untreated as he refused to accept the diagnosis or medicate for the condition. He is buried at Rockwood Cemetery next to The Royal North Shore hospital.

I felt honoured to meet Thelma. I felt a kinship and adored her openness and warmth.

A memory I will keep in my heart forever.

JACK, PATRICIA and GREG MULLINS

Patricia and Jack Mullins

Jack – War Veteran RAAF/Senior Work Supervisor, Department of Public Works NSW
Patricia – Primary School Teacher at Mimosa Public School
Greg – Former Fire and Rescue Commissioner NSW

Both Jack (1924–2018) and Patricia (1929–2008) were very active in the Terrey Hills Community, with Jack being valued as the "doer" and Patricia an incredible organiser.

Moving into the area in 1955, they were awarded one block of land in a returned service ballot at a reduced interest rate. Neither of them had even heard of Terrey Hills and set out to explore the area on their old Harley Davidson Motorcycle, with their three children, Terrey, Kim and Robin, riding along in the sidecar. Greg, their fourth child, was born in 1959.

(They sadly lost Terrey to a car accident in 1972).

Jack built a garage on the land, using his learned skills as a carpenter, which the family lived in while the main home was being built. It took many weekends dedicated to working on the build, and four years to complete, with the family moving into their new home in 1959.

They both relished the bushland surroundings and strong sense of community their family was now a part of.

The 1960s brought about tremendous change in the area for the Mullinses, with the installation of town water and the residential expansion. During these times, you were expected to have a role within your community. The Deputy Shire President at the time, Frank Beckman (later to become a lifelong friend of Jack's), knocked on the door to welcome them into the area but his intentions were also of the "announcement" variety, proclaiming everyone pulled their weight in the area and that they needed to think about what they were willing to contribute to.

One might speak of someone "building" a community but both Jack and Patricia took this to an entirely new level, with Jack having actually helped build extensions for the Terrey Hills RFS station and extend the community centre, along with coaching the local rugby union teams and being an active member of the school P&C, The Red Cross and The Progress Association communities.

Meanwhile, Patricia coordinated volunteer bush regeneration programs, managed the Eramboo Adult Education Group and was also respected as an active member of the P&C, The Red Cross and The Progress Association (in which they were both awarded Life Membership).

Jack also volunteered for the local Fire Brigade, later becoming the Terrey Hills Department Deputy Captain, helping to protect the area from fires in 1957, 1968 and 1979 (said to be the worst of them all), continuing as a volunteer firefighter for fifty years. He was awarded a Long Service Award for his contributions to firefighting.

* * * *

Their fourth child, Greg Mullins, respectfully continued the legacy of his father volunteering alongside his dad since the age of 12.

After many years of service, Greg was awarded the prestigious title of The New South Wales Fire and Rescue Commissioner, a title he successfully attained for years (the second longest serving commissioner in history).

The photo of Jack in the plane is of him flying at 92 years old, after not having been in a fighter since the war.

After two decades of fighting fires, Greg resigned in 2017 to concentrate on climate issues. He says he re-joined The Terrey Hills Fire Brigade upon retirement, "Because it was very special to me that Dad and I had fought so many fires together."

With each of them possessing incredible community spirit, bravery, morals and an aim for protection of humanity and community, and with their work in the aforementioned fields – along with anti-war, indigenous rights, women's rights and the protection of the environment – Jack, Patricia and Greg are celebrated for creating a close, caring and connected community.

Fire chief retiring

State head has served 13 years as commissioner

John Morcombe

FIRE & Rescue NSW Commissioner Greg Mullins has announced he will step down from the role in January.

The Cromer resident is the state's longest-serving urban fire service chief since 1898.

He is the first person to come from the ranks to fill the role of both chief fire officer and chief executive officer

Mr Mullins started as a recruit with what was then called the NSW Fire Brigade in 1978 after having served as a bushfire brigade volunteer for six years.

His father Jack has been a member of the Terrey Hills RFS for 61 years and is a life member.

Mr Mullins said he was hanging up his helmet to hand over the reins to someone with new ideas, passion and the energy to take Fire & Rescue NSW into its next chapter.

"It has been an enormous privilege to serve beside incredibly dedicated men and women who willingly put their own lives on the line on

Fire & Rescue NSW Commissioner Greg Mullins is retiring.

a daily basis to save people who they have never met," he said.

"While I know that my last day will be very sad for me and my family, I also know that the brigade is in excellent hands and will continue to provide outstanding service to the community.

"I've done the best I can over the past 13 years as commissioner and it has been immensely rewarding

but I'm looking forward to spending more time with family and not being on call 24/7."

Mr Mullins' path through Fire & Rescue included 10 years as an elected union official and a masters degree in management. He is a graduate of the Institute of Company Directors, a graduate of the United States Fire Academy and Oxford Strategic Leadership Program.

The Terrey Hills Rural Fire Brigade marks its 70th birthday on Wednesday. Jack Mullins has been with them for 57 years. Picture: VIRGINIA YOUNG

Passion to serve still burns brightly

John Morcombe

THE Terrey Hills Rural Fire Brigade celebrates its 70th birthday today and Jack Mullins has been there for 57 of those years.

Not that life member Mr Mullins, 87, has to travel far to the station — he only lives 500m away down Yulong Rd.

"I used to rush up the road when the siren sounded," he said. "When we moved here in October 1955, it was a very rural area and people were expected to join at least one of the local organisations."

Mr Mullins passed the passion to serve to his son Greg, who began as a RFS volunteer and is now the commissioner of Fire and Rescue NSW.

The first meeting of the Terrey Hills Volunteer Bush Fire Brigade, as it was then called, was held in the one-room school at Terrey Hills on December 12, 1942. In February, 1943, the brigade asked Warringah Council for some equipment.

Soon the brigade was equipped with a few burners, scrub hooks, knapsacks and a portable siren.

By late 1944, the brigade had 40 members but it was not until 1956 that it got its first truck — a Chevrolet Blitz tanker that could carry nearly 3000 litres of water.

"It's a terrific brigade — it's one of the best — and we've always had very good response times," Mr Mullins said. "I'm 88 this month and I can't do a lot now so they keep me as an emergency driver."

RICHARD FRIAR + WENDY HARPER

Wendy (born 1960) – Holistic Medicine, Film-maker, Writer/Poet, Peace, Humanity and Sustainability Advocate.
Richard (1944–2019) – Artist, Film-maker, Voice for Sustainable Living and First-Time Big Wave Surfer Pioneer in Europe.

Ric grew up on the Northern Beaches, although his parents originated from the UK. When he was four, the family moved from their hometown of Kent in England to start a new life in Australia.

Life wasn't easy for Ric as he was left-handed and dyslexic. He was often punished at school with the cane to his left hand in an attempt to encourage him to use his right hand. Home life wasn't a nurturing environment for Ric either, so he took to surfing and going to the movies for escapism. He lived his life as if it were a movie. The world was his stage.

As Ric continued into his adult life, his instincts would come to outweigh his basic education and become his beacon. "Instinct will tell you how to live your purpose." – Quote from the late Ric Friar.

With his faith in following this theory, and living on instinct, he became the very first board-rider to brave the thirty-foot waves at The Cribbar, in the UK, more commonly known as "The Widow Maker".

In 1966 and twenty-two years old, Ric was living in England, acting and hobnobbing with the likes of supermodel, Twiggy. Ric was about to start acting the role of King Arthur in a London play when he decided to stop en-route to London, at Towan Head, and take in the magnificent sea.

Ric was taken by the mist, the noise and the beauty of the rolling waves in the sun. He had never seen anything quite like it. These waves had literally never been surfed before until the day Ric Friar stopped on the side of the road to get a glimpse of the ocean. Moments later, he was immersed in the depths of this very sea. Upon hearing that Ric was going to surf "The Cribbar", three others decided to join him. With no wetsuits, leg-ropes or double fins, this was a serious, life-threatening feat. Surviving the Tsunami-like waves, Ric left that surf, albeit with a smashed-up surfboard and disorientation, as the pioneer of big wave surfing in Europe.

Earlier, on Christmas Day 1963, he had surfed the freak 25-foot waves back in Newport, Australia, dislocating his shoulder and nearly drowning. He was washed up on the beach quite miraculously. "It was the most pleasant death I ever had." – Quote by Ric Friar.

Moving on to greener pastures, in the early 1990s, Ric was given the title of "King of Poo'" by a columnist in the Sydney Morning Herald for his pioneered use of manure, worms and mulch in horticulture. In 2009, Ric was given permission by the NSW Department of Primary Industries to study the possible commercialisation of hemp.

One fateful day in 1997, he met Wendy Harper. The two resided in Terrey Hills as they required land to continue the permaculture work of hemp farming and worm casting. They met and were married within weeks. They had their daughter, Honey Soul, in 1999.

Wendy spent the majority of the early-to-mid 80s as a home-birth midwife. She was integral in bringing expectant mothers' grassroots support through "skilled birth support", now known as the Doula Method.

During the same time, Wendy co-founded The Health Care Centre, which sought to give both doctors and patients of holistic medicine rights and a firm respectable place within the realm of practising medicine.

In 1987, Wendy was asked to join a friend in co-ordinating the EAT project (Ethiopia Aid Tonight) rock concert at The Sydney Opera House. The event raised over $1.5 million in famine relief for Ethiopia.

Her philanthropic work of conscience ethical living remains strong today as she pushes forward into new projects, including supporting her own local community through COVID kindness initiatives, such as housing over twenty international travellers during the time, to engineering a program focused on women's rights. Wendy is also a proud probationary member of the Terrey Hills Royal Fire Service.

Educating through the arts had also been a passion for both Wendy and Ric over their twenty years together. From 2007, subjects such as the anti-war movement, Australian Indigenous rights, railway history and more recently, the push to use a collaborative approach to women and men living in harmony, have all been documented. The pair have combined their passions for life, peace and sustainability through art, poetry, film and voice.

With the sad passing of Ric late in 2019, Wendy is left to continue the legacy and bring voice to meaningful matters.

The Farmhouse

Renovation

When renovating The Farmhouse, one of the first rooms to be designed was that of the Mudroom. With the family of six (including four boys), flower cutting from the garden and creating floral arrangements, keeping chickens, horses and owning a dog, we required a big and beautiful space to carry out daily farmhouse chores.

Everyday jobs like washing clothes, cleaning, collecting eggs and tending to the animals and garden are made all that more enjoyable within this open and pretty space.

In designing the kitchen, the hope was to envelope the atmosphere of a cooking and eating space as you would find in a traditional Italian "Masseria".

Our family has been lucky enough to enjoy many trips to rural Italy over the years and enjoyed the feeling of Famiglia. To ensure authenticity in giving a nod to not only the memories of our travels, but also to the history of the area in which The Farmhouse resides, included in the design are Italian handmade wall tiles, traditionally rendered surfaces, Italian appliances, a hand-painted Italian mural and an internal wood-burning pizza oven.

A kitchen is often described as the heart of the home but this one beats louder than most.

To complement these elements and create a unique space with eclecticism, we included the addition of a 100-year-old cast iron farmhouse sink from the USA, a restored vintage Aga oven (you can't have a Farmhouse without an Aga!) from eBay, antique furniture and art and an original French chandelier.

Soft natural hues of green and blue – along with natural surfaces such as reclaimed wood – complement highly polished inclusions such as stainless steel bench-tops and the strong accent of black solidifies an air of robust masculinity to the space.

The ceiling is a unique feature especially in the Australian city of Sydney! The wood was discovered by the builder on a property in the Blue Mountains, roughly milled to keep its authenticity and installed in the kitchen. The height of the ceilings was lowered to create an emotive space of nurture and warmth.

Whether it's pizza dough being rolled out on the hand-poured cement-topped island benchtop, records spinning on the LP player, morning or afternoon cuddles with the family dog taking place in the nook or the custom-made round table filled with food and family (or all at once), this kitchen "room" could not be more successful in both its execution and function.

Even though food and drinks are mainly enjoyed in the kitchen, the formal dining area is a favourite place to gather.

Inspiration for this room came from the private dining area you may see at a beautiful country house hotel. The moody palette – with black painted walls, dark timber, along with the stone floors and a raised real wood fireplace – ensure an environment set for cosy feasts.

The table was handmade by an architectural salvage warehouse in Sydney using random timber cuts-offs that were destined for the tip. They were carefully collected off the floor and curated to create this beauty seating up to twenty-four people at a time if needed.

An earthy but sophisticated approach to the master bedroom. Wood, stones, linens and an abundance of natural light.

The fireplace is clad in individually chosen, cut and placed real river stones. A commissioned piece by Sydney artist Paul Ryan hangs on the fireplace, a 20th anniversary present I gifted to my husband, taking pride of place within the room.

Antique leather rocker and French art student oil were purchased at the Art and Antique Fair in Sydney.

Continuing the earthy colour palette of the master bedroom, the master bath engages a combination of natural wood, steel, horns and antique textiles.

A nod to the earlier Italian residents of the area is evoked with an antique oil portrait of a Catholic nun and a pretty Italian antique lace tablecloth was repurposed into a delicate window treatment.

The walls are treated with a tiny meadow flower printed wallpaper in a soft blue and white to create an air of femininity.

The free-standing washbasin is a combination of locally sourced antiques.

The mint green enamel sink was dropped into the free-standing wooden table to make as one. The table was salvaged and once belonged to The Periwinkle in Manly before it was knocked down.

Being that The Farmhouse is situated in an enormously equestrian heavy area, reference is made to horses in the area throughout the interior design.

A wonderful vintage find of these up-cycled riding boots made for fabulous bedside lamps. With the lamps and one of the children's own artworks of an abstract painted chicken, framed and positioned in pride of place above the bed, the interiors of this bedroom remind you of your surrounds.

Everyone's favourite room in the house: the den.

In here, pool tournaments and dart competitions are held, family movie nights are enjoyed and late night post-dinner-party soirees always see this room filled with friends and family.

Giving reference to the equestrian culture of the area, the walls have been peppered with an antique toile patterned wallpaper of riding scenes and layered with vintage oil paintings and photographs in the same theme.

The space is an organised, diverse collection of hats, Wellington boots, firewood, riding helmets, umbrellas, books and sporting equipment.

To the right as you enter the Farmhouse, the library is visible with shelves bursting with books. Feel the welcome crackle from the open fire in the cooler months.

Taking the lead from European farmhouses, an organic rendered finish was applied to the exterior walls and painted white. The most trusted, generational

Italian family-owned render company was asked to do the work to ensure authenticity and quality.

These cane egg chairs were actually a roadside find that were restored to their former glory.

The cane egg chairs make for a great hide-away on the back verandah to watch the magical sunsets at The Farmhouse

Fabric

Nature uses only the longest threads to weave her patterns, so that each small piece of her fabric reveals the organisation of the entire tapestry.

~ Richard Feynman

The sheer drapery in the bathroom was imagined from an antique lace tablecloth.

It gives the space an authentic Italian masseria vibe.

Brass and copper tapware fittings were installed throughout The Farmhouse. As they patina, the pieces will beautify with time and look as if they were part of an age-old original Farmhouse.

Wallpaper is also a common feature throughout The Farmhouse. The addition of traditional papers gives the rooms a nostalgic style.

Lighting

The featured lighting in The Farmhouse is a curated collection of antique and barn finds from our family travels throughout Italy and the United States.

The original Italian Murano lighting was acquired at a village street market in Puglia and the more American styled fixtures were found in various barns in Vermont, USA.

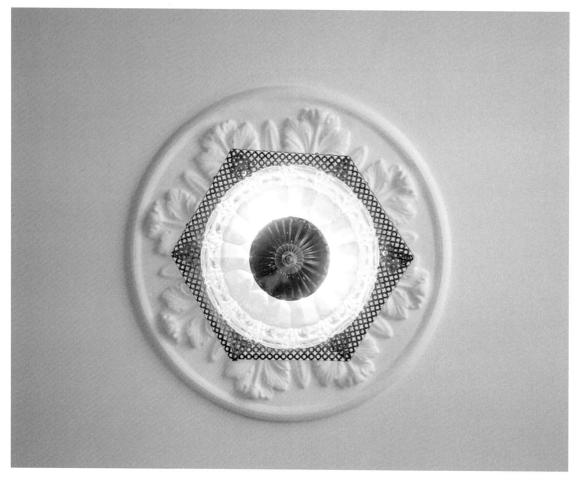

Surfaces

Textures, prints, antiques and vintage finds – along with collectively displaying treasures, keepsakes and meaningful art – all make up the fabric of The Farmhouse.

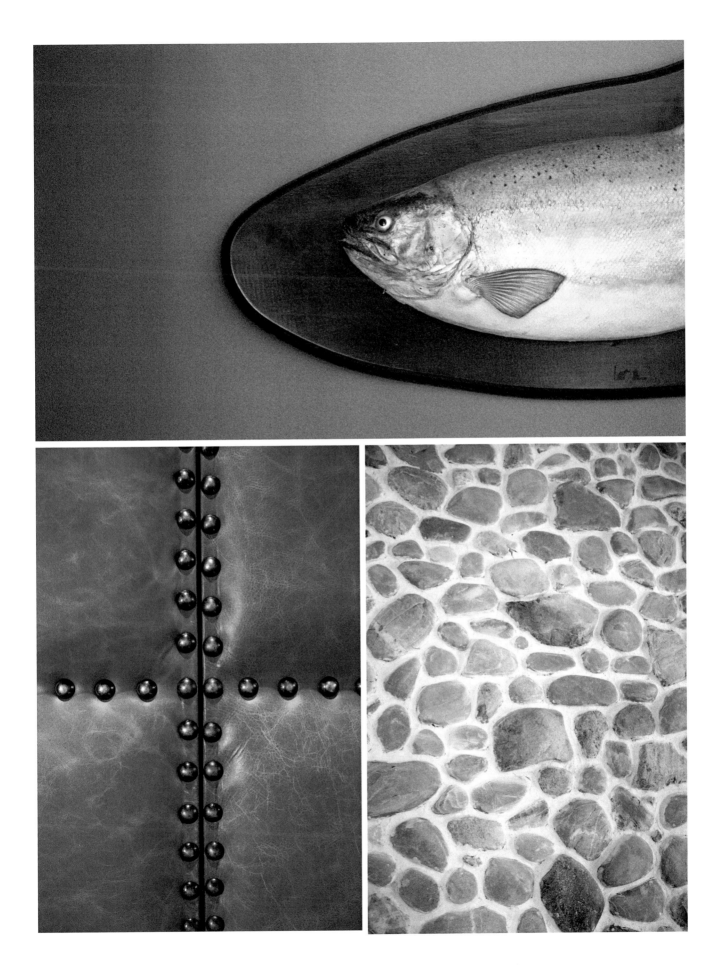

Wallpaper

When designing The Farmhouse, there was constant reference to the prevalent equestrian involvement in the area. Papers were sourced from France and Italy with beautiful motifs and toiles du jour images of horseback riding.

Functionality

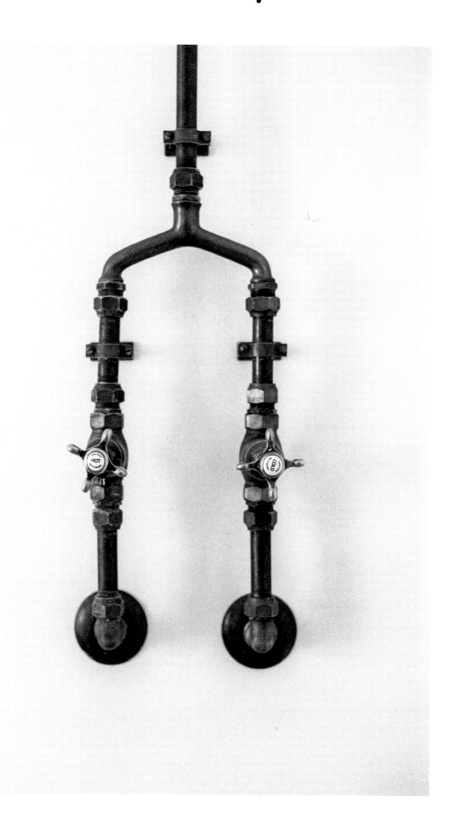

Collected over the years, copper pots and pans get used regularly.

The AGA oven was purchased on eBay and restored by a local restorer from The Mountains.

In Winter, the oven stays on permanently. Slow-cooked dishes and soups are often bubbling away.

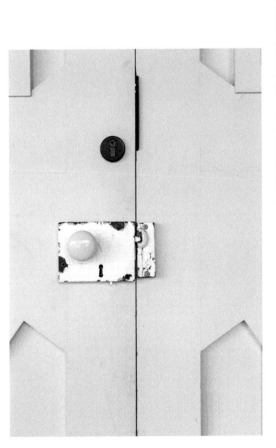

Wood Fired Oven pizza tools hand made for The Farmhouse.

W. KARL BROWN

TERREY HILLS LIBRARY

William Karl Brown (always known as Karl Brown) was born 6/10/1891, died 30/8/1981, in his 90th year.

He received an Award from "Warringah Shire Council in 1974 for 38 years of faithful Service rendered to the Community, as Foundation member of the Terrey Hills Volunteer Bushfire Brigade and local Parents and Citizens Association and for Services given as Librarian and Secretary of the Terrey Hills Library."

Karl joined the Terrey Hills Library in 1961.
In 1963, at the age of 72, he learned the Dewey System of classifying books and taught this to the other volunteer Librarians.
He catalogued the non fiction books (over 2,000), and covered many of them until he relinquished the task of cataloguer in April 1978. He remained a member of the Committee until 1979. He was elected a life member in 1980.

Written by his loving daughter,

Elaine Mullin
E.I.Mullin
14th October, 2005.

W.Karl Brown was born in England to a poor working class family.
He had very little schooling. He started work at about 9 years of age delivering brightly coloured pots. He was allowed 1 farthing a week which he kept under the carpet. He loaned money to his Father on Saturdays to retrieve his suit from the Pawnbroker so he could wear it to Church on Sundays. On Mondays his father returned his money and the suit to the Pawnbroker.

He persuaded his sister and 2 brothers to contribute so that he could buy a second-hand Dictionary for his Mother's Birthday. It cost 6 pence.
His sister later told me that his mother seldom opened it , but that Karl almost wore it out. From this stemmed his lifelong love of books.

After serving in World War 1, Karl met and married a very well educated Lady, Faye Carver, and they had four children. With her help, and life, and books, he lived a very full, happy, and constructive life. That is another Story!

Elaine Mullin.   14/10/05.

Everything we are and do is only temporary. We are only here for such a short period of time to learn, grow and make our own unique imprint on Mother Earth. Our time and efforts within our living environment hopefully elevate the space, preparing it in a positive manner for the next fateful inhabitant.

I take care in making sure our time here as visitors and a family at The Farmhouse is being spent fruitfully, with purpose and a solid injection of love, family values, and respect for the land. Adding creativity in spades and learning about our ancestors and their success in longevity of daily practice, such as farming, has also been poignant in our growth and preparing the property for others to enjoy for years to come. I see it as kind of like passing the baton. Every time I plant a new species or create a new space, I am acutely aware of the future. I hope in doing so, in some small way, our own contribution here at The Farmhouse is adding another positive layer to the process.

I also hope you have been inspired by this book, and you too are able to see, whatever you choose to put your heart and soul into, it's something you are building for generations to come. You are leaving a legacy.

Thank you for taking the time to read my book. It is very much appreciated, and I hope you were able to take away something unique and inspiring from it.